ANDRÉ MALRAUX

Past Present Future

ANDRÉ MALRAUX

Past Present Future

Conversations with Guy Suarès

THAMES AND HUDSON · LONDON

For my daughters, Marika, Annabelle, Dominique

Guy Suarès

General Editor: Claude Glayman
Photographic Reportage: Daniel Pype
Graphic Designer: Roman Cieslewicz

©1974 Editions Stock, Paris
First published in France under the title *Malraux, Celui Qui Vient*
English translation by Derek Coltman © 1974 Thames and Hudson,
London

Printed and bound in France

ISBN 0 500 23211 3

CONTENTS

André Malraux, Guy Suarès, José Bergamín

Conversations

Conversations   1973

The Alps, Switzerland
January 1973

Night is about to fall: definitive darkness. Opaque silence from which expectation wells in constant rebirth. For hours now the snow has not stopped falling, a kaleidoscope whose every particle is rhythm, colour, and Miloscz's "sterile meditation of silence with the wan thought of the moon its perpetual conclusion".

There was a time, and this moment is a retrospective witness to it, when night was fecundating the day, and when the roughness of sand enveloped a marvelling adolescent in its warmth as he gazed, untiring, while the foam on an infinite shore brightened with its snow the beaches of that America which Claudel was to discover as Louis Laine and christen as Don Rodrigue.

"I fly in the air like a buzzard, like Jean-le-Blanc
hovering on high!
And I see the earth appear beneath the sun's
flames, and I hear
The crack of illumination reach
The earth beneath the sun's splendour, and the
rivers flowing where the great boss of its body
dictates . . ."

My expectation then was no less than tonight's. January of fire. January of ice. But the silence of that new world was filled with calling voices and I knew that I had a choice to make, I knew that I was going to perform my first act as a man, an act that would abolish forever a certain form of mystery, since to choose also means to renounce all other possibles. "What perfect voice" will tell the truth of the corn to be reaped, in this winter night of 1973? Can that voice still be heard? Does it exist? And if it does exist, will it assent to speak to this shifting image of myself in which I see my past, my present, my future, all indivisibly reflected? But if that voice did not exist, if it had never been raised in the world, what meaning could my expectation have? From the sterilized darkness images begin to emerge. The voices that have always called to us become more urgent. The voices whose names are Rilke, Miloscz, Lorca, Bergamín, Claudel, Alberti, Neruda. And others, many others, now sounding loud in our ears, now moving away, only to return with still more insistent rhythm, a still more persuasive presence. The voice raised tonight drowns them all. What silence suddenly surrounds it! It sounds in my ears as it did on that day between the ocean and the pines buffeted by the wind and spray. Still faithful to itself, telling me tirelessly as ever about the Human Condition, its shattered Hope, its lucid Conquerors, where on the Royal Way the Voices of Silence and the Metamorphosis of the Gods once planted those Fallen Oaks.

January 30, 1973

Dear André Malraux, it was not without "fear and trembling" that I undertook this book-film of your life and action. I owe it to myself to keep my doubts in the face of this ambitious enterprise to myself, but I cannot resist communicating to you the exaltation that re-reading your works has brought me. Living again through your *Tentation de l'Occident, Les Conquérants, Le Triangle noir*, is a journey back to the wellsprings, and I am filled with wonder as I realize how deeply all those works left their mark on me, and why I am approaching you now, in my fortieth year, with such breathless anticipation, with such hope. You could well reply, and rightly, that your work itself is still there (and oh, how filled with life!), and that it was woven into the woof of time by the deeds and words that combined to prolong and perfect its dimension. That is only too true. But who, if not you and you alone, is capable of restoring "its meaning and its purpose" to my generation, the generation now reaching its noon. What strikes me above all is that there is no dichotomy between your life and your work. Something that is not always the case, if we think of Rodin, Rilke, Claudel, among others. Though I intend no judgment by the distinction. From your first visit to Indochina to the Spanish Civil War, from the Resistance to your long march at the side of General de Gaulle, always the same anguish, the same tension, the same lucidity. I still do not know what form our meetings are to take, or how to formulate my sense of expectation into concrete questions. But since anguish and expectation are so strong, you will know, I have no doubt, how best to answer them . . .

I know now, since this morning, that my call has been heard, and that the man who has answered it will not fail the myth with which my youth has constantly kept faith. My expectation has been granted a precise, lucid, unequivocal reply, one that reveals in the man who made it a receptive power composed equally of modesty and generosity. I shall have to go straight for my goal. Make sure of my aim. Not disappoint him. But the sun is rising in the distance and thinning the mists of the winter night. As I gaze at the postcard Alps outside, I feel a need to transpose, to see instead the ragged ridge of the Andes, the *cordillera* whose harsh beauty still pursues me. "Realm of fervour, whatever your ancient fame and your high birth, there comes an hour when the wound you bear in your heart can no longer be hid and bleeds afresh. The hour of gravest silence." Will André Malraux break that silence? When the privileged moment arrives, I must listen to that silence, let myself sink slowly into its depths. Listen to the silence in myself and allow it to winnow, to trim, to mould my expectation.

Fernand Malraux, his father

June 10, 1973

Our first meeting is fixed for four this afternoon. The car moves at processional speed, a painful crawl. I attempt to take a last glance through the plan for this first interview, fully aware as I do so that life and the reality of a human presence will defeat all the snares I may have laid for them. Soon I shall have to throw away my crutches. Here I am on the little road leading to Verrières. On one side the fields, or what is left of them. On the other a grey stone wall, the colour of time. The car slows down and enters a courtyard. At the far side of it, clearly outlined, stands the old house exuding a melancholy charm. I can't help thinking of Chekhov and his *Cherry Orchard*. A Cherry Orchard that has somehow managed to escape the assaults of time. Inside the front door a strange silence reigns. A full, attentive silence. I know that our host will appear at four o'clock, and we move on into the drawing-room, where the furniture, the paintings, the objets d'art are conjuring up memories, presences, muffled conversations, among themselves, for themselves. How comforting, those mysterious emanations from the past. There is a little Braque leaning against a lamp. I am staggered as it impinges on me how perfectly it succeeds in marrying past with present. A fishing boat washed up here, still battered by ocean spray and storm. The canvas lights up everything around it, a justification of the past in its justification of the present. It casts a magic spell, and the metamorphosis turning it into a timeless and therefore classic canvas has already begun.

While I examined the room, the sound and photographic crews were setting up their lamps, their wires, and an odd parasol affair that, when duly lit up, was to enable our first interview to be "filmed". Then the unpredictable made its first irruption. The tape broke, and all the lamps blew. I could only offer up thanks to life for recalling me so brutally to reality, and recall Georges Dullin, the great actor-manager, shaking his fist at the iron safety curtain of his theater, the Atelier, one first night when it refused to wind up, and yelling: "Betrayed by machines! Betrayed by the machines!" It was a Monday and everywhere was closed. Daniel Pype, galvanized by despair, charged down into Verrières and returned most unexpectedly with ten replacement bulbs, of which the first nine also promptly blew, and the tenth, insanely but fortunately, survived. It was four o'clock. André Malraux was there. We hadn't seen him come in.

The last time I had seen him was in September 1968. Just back from Latin America, I had gone to give him an account of what we had managed to accomplish in Brazil, in Uruguay, Argentina, and Chile. Pablo Neruda had asked me to convey to Malraux the joy it would

< André Malraux, aged 8, in the centre of a beach group (1910)

André Malraux at 14; in the centre, Mademoiselle Paulette Thouvenin

16

give him to see an exhibition of the Easter Island gods organized in Paris.

Beneath the Minister of Culture's extraordinary capacity to make one welcome, I had sensed then a certain underlying tension. Was it the presentiment that a phase of action was drawing to an end? An awareness of already possessing a less than total grasp upon history and its derisions? The furnishings, there on the Rue de Valois, were reverting to blank official-dom, a stage setting about to lose its credibility. He surely knew as much. But now, in Verrières, because we neither of us embarrassed the other with polite formalities, our meeting seemed to discover a sort of self-justifying urgency the moment we were once more face to face.

"When you were twenty, did you have a plan? If so, what was it?"

"The plan was a life *outside life*; something to which art was to make a tremendous contribution. And also, parallel to that, the discovery of another world, another civilization. Hence Asia. The feeling I had about the existence of different worlds was quasi-organic. And another world, in 1921, took the form of another civilization. Asia today is a tourist attraction, in those days it still had mystery. And the mystery of alien civilizations was certainly linked to that of civilizations past and gone.

"The first time I met him, Valéry asked me: what did you go to China for? My answer then was the same one I have just given you. On reflection, I have since come to the conclusion that I probably sensed the difference between civilizations, between their mental structures, as a notion fundamental to the understanding of man. If you like, I experienced this difference I sensed as an essential mystery of the civilization in which I was born.

"I'm afraid conversation is not as precise as the written word; I am obliged to use the word civilization both in the sense we give it in 'Greek civilization' and also in the sense in which it signifies the history and totality of civilizations generally. The context will make it clear no doubt . . ."

"The events that have marked the past sixty years have also toppled a number of previously accepted basic facts. What is your feeling about the world today?"

"Firstly, that it is transient. When I was twenty we had a great tendency, despite the 1914–18 war, to believe in a world that was like a single plant, just continuing its isolated vegetable life. A hundred years earlier, that tendency had been even more pronounced. Among eighteenth-century writers it was obviousness

< André Malraux with
Guy Suarès at
Verrières-le-Buisson,
June 10, 1973

Fernand Malraux

itself. After the Napoleonic wars everyone was aware of a mutation, whereas no one had been aware of the one that occurred in 1672. And even so, the nineteenth-century Romantic was not aware of any mutation in the actual nature of civilization. In *La Confession d'un enfant du siècle*, Musset tells us: our parents rode out to do battle, and here are we, just sitting in a café. But even then there still didn't exist the feeling *we* had of discovering a world very different from the one that had gone before it, a world that would probably be succeeded by another just as different again.

"So, the first answer to your question is: a violent sense of transience. And apart from that, I also experienced the feeling that this civilization of ours was unprecedented; unprecedented because it was the heir of all the others. Remember, we were the first. To someone of your generation the idea is banal; but it had never happened before. A civilization that starts talking about Sumeria, about Egypt, about India, Mexico, etc., as data among other data, the data on which our understanding of man must be founded, that was certainly the first time. The scope of human knowledge had been vastly extended, ethnography, ethnology, all sorts of things were being brought into play. Art was discovering reproduction, the totality of all these new techniques and kinds of knowledge was confronting us with civilizations whose very range presented an enigma; whereas our predecessors had lived in a privileged civilization, the Mediterranean civilization, and they looked upon all the others as more or less barbarian. For Hegel, and even for a Marxist (I remember, when I was in Russia the first time . . .), there is *a* History, History with a capital H, just as there is only one civilization."

"The Christian civilization? Or Judaeo-Christian?"

"Which culminated in Marx. The line of descent was Greece—Christianity—Hegelianism—Marxism. But we don't make any claims of that sort; we aren't prepared to try fitting Pre-Columbian art into a genealogy of that sort, or Chinese thought . . . And another characteristic peculiar to our civilization (though I was to discover this later) is that it has no accepted values. Almost all other civilizations have known what their values were."

He fell abruptly silent, and I had the strange impression of seeing him hurtling through centuries of chaos, wielding that gift of concision that leads him to the essence of things: to see clearly, to mould the irrational, to bring back into consciousness, and through it, a past that he has travelled and that must be used to explain our present.

"These values of ours, we know what they are, but

André Malraux aged 4

3

André Malraux . . . the young musketeer

they seem to have been emptied of their substance. Their dynamic force has been disconnected, their unity shattered, so that we no longer recognize them as values at all.

"A Christian in the eighteenth century could distinguish quite clearly between good and evil. In our day, thinking about the values of our civilization entails an investigation of what they are, whereas in the past there was never any question of inquiring into the values by which you lived. Which is even more striking when you think that though there have been other civilizations, very few — perhaps the late Roman Empire — with weak values, they were all dying civilizations. Whereas the civilization in which we find ourselves, whose values we feel to be either dying or still to be born, is the most powerful civilization the world has ever known."

"Isn't there something of a paradox there?"

"Yes. And I expressed it once by saying: what is the good of going to the moon if it's just to commit suicide there? Yet the fact remains that we are capable of going to the moon . . .

"Now let's get on to the third characteristic. The first: a civilization without precedent. Second: one without recognized values. Third: a civilization cut off from the cosmos. Greek civilization is inseparable from the fact that it was linked to the cosmos by its gods. Any Greek god you care to name is a mediator between the cosmos and man via a specific group of natural forces. For example: Man-love and even fertility; Aphrodite-the cosmos. The Middle Ages experienced this continuity in a completely different way, but still very strongly. God made the evening and the morning, and good Christian folk were linked to their God by the bells that rang them in. The Angelus was a time of day, but it was also the Angel of the Annunciation. And apart from that, Christianity is a religion in which commemorations have played a decisive rôle. A Christianity without Christmas is inconceivable. And though Christ's birth was a unique event, that event is reproduced by every commemoration of it. Christian civilization at its height provided very strong links between man and the Christian cosmos. Whereas our civilization no longer has any Aphrodite, or even any profound commemorations: the fourteenth of July is hardly Christmas — or even the Angelus. Though it's true that our civilization does have one conscious link with the cosmos — of a very different sort, but a link all the same. I mean its action upon the natural world, particularly in the Communist world, in what we might call the Marxist civilization. The Russians of the great revolutionary era certainly felt a bond between themselves and the earth: man must conquer the earth for the good of all mankind. A Marxist society postulates an end to social

25

injustice achieved by the triumph of the proletariat; then, in the resulting world of equality, pioneers will go out to conquer the earth and bring back to all whatever they succeed in winning from it. Perhaps that is a contemporary form of what was once man's dialogue with the cosmos."

"Don't you have the feeling that our Western civilization is coming to the end of a seemingly ineluctable decadence? I can't help being reminded of the great declines that overtook so many ancient civilizations: Egypt, Greece, China, among others. If you share that feeling, do you think our civilization may be able to make a fresh start with the help of transfusions from outside, perhaps in the form of some new or old mystique or philosophy?"

"We are to some extent back with the previous question here. Because basically your question springs from a Spenglerian conception of successive cultures. Each civilization is an organism, civilizations are similar organisms, New York is the heir of Alexandria and Byzantium, the death throes of any civilization create the vast cosmopolitan cities that are the symptoms of its death, etc. But if you look at all those previous civilizations Spengler and Toynbee studied — they call them cultures — you will notice that not one of them has been the heir of all the others before it, whereas that is the very definition of ours. Perhaps Byzantium and New York are the same thing, yet Byzantium never gave a thought to Alexandria, whereas we are only too conscious of Byzantium. Our need to study all the earth's civilizations poses a problem without precedent. First of all, in the domain of art.

"Is the relation of our civilization to its values bound to give birth, sooner or later, to a new religion? It is a possible supposition. But the idea only becomes really interesting if we ask: in what form? To begin with, a new religion is not inevitably the renewal of an old one. It can be, and there could be a new Christianity. But not inevitably. It can also have nothing much in common with its predecessors at all. Religions have been unified into a phenomenology, but it isn't true that Christianity is 'the same thing' as paganism, that both belong in a common domain. It's not like that at all. When paganism was dying, at the end of the Roman Empire, the philosophers in Baiae predicted that its heir would be Stoicism. Only the heir turned out in the event to be Christianity, and the philosophers had scarcely given that a thought. So there's nothing to stop us supposing that any religious rebirth might be based on different data from the ones we assume. Even within a phenomenology, our religious feeling is a Christian one, and it is quite possible to postulate a religion alien to the fundamental elements of Christianity."

< Fernand Malraux

André Malraux and his father (1917)

28

203

< André Malraux, aged 8 (1910)

André Malraux at 21

Silence. He seemed suddenly to be contemplating within himself a vast fresco of uncertain yet terribly present shadows. He listened, and I with him, to all man's successive hopes, his tirelessly renewed quests for a truth that would hold firm. But truth has seventeen layers, like an onion, as the saying goes. He gazed out at the great park in the distance, where a rainy June was bringing a second spring. An infinite spectrum of greens exchanging bright challenges, indifferent to the sound and fury of the octopus city as it crushed and ground its inhabitants against the harsh events of their lives only a few kilometres away.

"Are there still events for you? And if so, which are the ones that seem to you most important?"

"Number one, quite clearly, must be the atomic bomb. But certain major facts of our time are not events at all. For example, our whole questioning of the basis of civilization, which is something that has never existed before to such a degree, that has never really existed at all. A few small groups have wondered what was going to happen, but all the same no one announced the end of Rome. St. Augustine discusses it very seriously, but by that time Rome had in fact fallen. Whereas today, we are conscious that civilization is in crisis, that its foundations are being questioned; but that is not an event."

"You said to Jean-Marie Domenach: 'The absurd has been used as an answer. In fact it was a question.' Do you still stand by that?"

"Completely. The absurd, as you know, has achieved international celebrity. I was talking earlier about the fundamental feeling of Difference. In my view, the absurd is that feeling of Difference experienced negatively, experienced as angst and pain. It could be experienced with indifference, it could be experienced with exaltation, as multiplicity, plurality (a sort of Hinduism, except that transmigration reintegrates the Hindu multiplicity into unity . . .), and it can be experienced as a tragic conflict. Our civilization, without any doubt, has experienced it as such a conflict, and extracted from it the myth of the absurd. The absurd, in short, is the consciousness of disharmony. I pointed out earlier that previous civilizations have all linked man in one way or another to the cosmos. Not only is the West not linked to the cosmos, it is also very shakily linked to any universal notion of Man and History. The door is closed. So we hurl ourselves at it hoping to break it down. Besides which, what has been written about the absurd postulates that man needs human consciousness to provide him with a justification of the universe; but that is by no means certain. The essential problems of our civilization, could they perhaps fade away temporarily — for two or three hundred years? A number of very important questions were deferred in the nineteenth century. For such a long time that people began to think, oh well, science can't resolve them, but it will later on . . ."

The shadow of Albert Camus was suddenly there between us. The comradely Camus of *The Myth of Sisyphus*. The despairing Camus of *The Fall*. From Mediterranean sun to night and its phantoms, Camus could claim the anguish in Malraux's *Walnut Trees of Altenburg* as his own: "We know that we did not choose to be born . . . That we did not choose our parents. That we have no power against time. That there exists between each one of us and the life of the universe a sort of . . . crevasse . . ."

"Crevasse", yes. Long before Greece, whose song Camus rediscovered, Israel was already raising its voice to the God of Justice and Wrath, seeking to slake its perpetually renewed spiritual expectation in wrath and fervour. Hasn't man always expected a justification of the universe from his consciousness? The man beside me knew better than anyone to what extent the human mind thinks man only in the eternal. And that "consciousness of life cannot be other than anguish". Those values he has lived out, made explicit, the values that have given his life a meaning which is now, with time, rising to the level of myth, how far will they be the values of tomorrow? I hesitated to put the question. There is such modesty in the man. And yet why had I come to him, why were we together at that moment, if not in order to stalk and try to grasp the essential?

"What is your hope for the future, as we now stand?"

"I have no idea, and I shall systematically eliminate all prophecy from our conversation."

The reply, admitting no rejoinder, came immediately.
He began glancing through the sheets of questions I had sent him, annotated now in red ink, in that vigorous writing mirroring perfectly the vivacity of a mind in perpetual motion. The slight surge of impatience over, he relaxed and went on:

"But you've made a note here that is probably the résumé of a question. Here it is: search for values — search for meaning. But to values and meaning we should also add chimeras . . . They are extremely important, because in the absence of religious faith imagination acquires tremendous power. Today we are faced with certain myths that, without being values, still manage to exercise a considerable influence. There is the myth of Democracy as understood in America,

During his military service

At Verrières, June 10, 1973 >

34

36

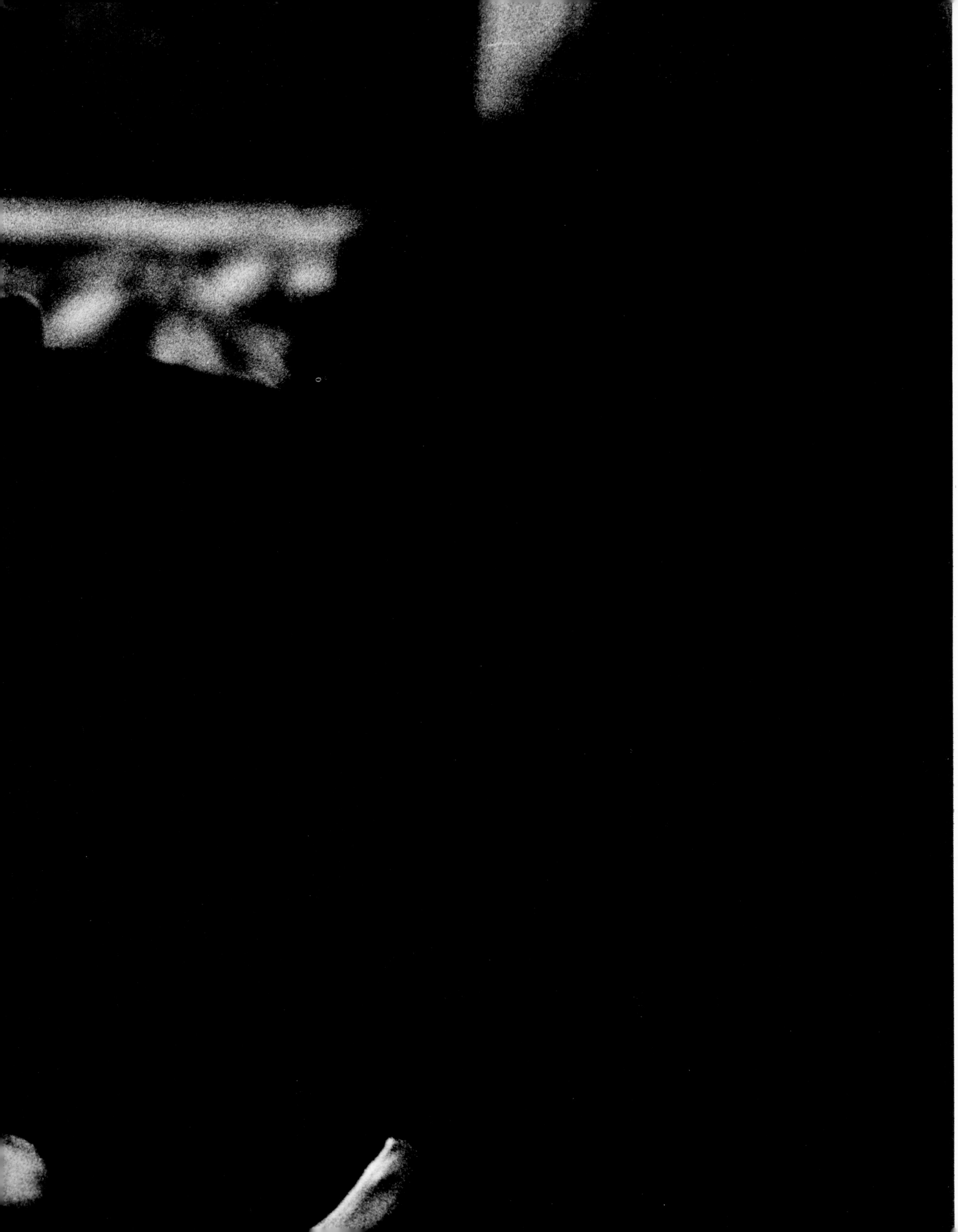

there is the myth of the Left as understood in France, and there is Nationalism. Are they secular religions? Not quite. Bizarre mythological constellations rather, that have succeeded in harnessing together a number of really rather diverse emotions, and as a result have achieved a considerable power of action. The 'May 1968' movement was a movement of young people throughout the entire world. Though the dates vary, there was a 'May 1968' in Japan, in California, in India, but nowhere involving people in their fifties; as with us in France, it was always the young."

Following his progress through life, I experience the same vertigo I have often felt when confronted with a painting by someone he probably admires: Vieira da Silva's *The Deck of Cards*. The same lucidity metamorphosed by form and colour into thought. Democracy, Socialism, Nationalism, all three had moulded our century when he was still not twenty years old. He had experienced them, lived through them with passion, those "chimeras", refusing all equivocations, cleaving resolutely to an ideal of action, preserving at the cost of whatever terrible struggles and risks were entailed a certain concept of the absolute. From what has been called his "Indochinese expedition", through the nightmare of Teruel, on to the comradeship of the Resistance, his path has always been one and the same, however multiple the human facets displayed on the way. A hero, it seemed to me, capable of revealing through that gift of brotherhood found flowering on battlefields what sainthood in our time could be. Today's lacerated, bewildered humanity has still gone on producing its saints and heroes, in concentration camps, on battlefields. 1917, 1936, 1940—45 had nothing in common with the various versions of May 1968. The great jubilee of '68 was tragic only in the lacks it revealed. The fragility of its myth transformed revolution into a psychodrama that has declined into derision.

"Could you define the hero, and the difference you establish between the hero and the saint? Do you see any connection between Job and Prometheus?"

"The hero and the saint when? And where? Roughly speaking, the hero is the man who stakes his life for the salvation of mankind. Though I'd like to bracket that phrase, so that salvation never gets left on its own. It is after all a religious word, and where Prometheus is concerned we would never say: the salvation of mankind; for mankind, certainly, but not salvation. The military hero isn't something we can just discard, because he has been an extremely powerful myth in his time; he doesn't bring salvation in the spiritual sense, he simply saves his followers from the enemy."

Clara and André Malraux
in Indochina (1923)

"So what differentiates him from the saint?"

"The hero is not defined by a transcendence, whereas the saint is inconceivable without transcendence. There can be no saint without a god. Admittedly the god doesn't have to be the Creator, or whatever you like to call him; but it comes to this: there can be no saint without human submission to a supreme value, and a transcendent supreme value. Whereas for the hero the problem of transcendence doesn't arise. Of course we can say that the nation is not like an individual, but we don't claim that national transcendence is quite on that level."

"What is saintliness? Would you say that there is any difference between saints such as St. John, St. Francis of Assisi, St. Bernard, and a character such as Job in the Old Testament?"

"Let's take the New first . . . Your last two, St. Francis and St. Bernard, are not only illustrious saints, they are also men who had an overwhelming effect upon art, whereas, and this is worth noting, there have been very great saints indeed, St. Paul for example, without any direct influence — his influence on Protestantism was of a different nature — whereas St. Francis . . .! Tuscan painting before and after are quite different, and St. Bernard, he is the whole Cistercian movement . . . Those particular saints, as opposed to St. Thomas and St. Augustine, owe their particular quality to the combination of their saintliness with their influence on artistic representation. Besides which, St. Francis of Assisi is the last of the very great saints, and the last of the great founders of Orders . . . Though you can sense immediately that Carmel isn't Franciscan. Christianity itself became Franciscan. Not only is the Christ of Chartres Franciscan, but even people's feelings begin to take on a particular colour . . . as though Christianity had quite suddenly become converted to Christ. The movements that made their influence felt through the monasteries seem to me to have no connection with those that changed Christian sensibility. And not only Christian sensibility: you find related phenomena in Buddhism. But perhaps I am influenced too much by art. You spoke of the Old Testament too."

"Yes. When I re-read Job's dialogues, David's psalms, Isaiah's prophecies, I can't help feeling how far their sense of expectancy, the fundamental lacuna they convey, lays a duty on man and on his God to close the great gap that keeps them apart. I feel that both God and man are realizing, sometimes in anger and rebellion, sometimes in tenderness and panic, the extent to which both are being summoned to saintliness. Does Job's saintliness differ from that of St. Francis?"

At Pnom Penh, 1923

"Job, David, Isaiah, they all lack what made St. Francis what he was: a spiritual transformation of the world. The saints achieved great importance in Christianity once they had come to constitute a sort of intercessory polytheism. There was Christ, then the Virgin Mary, then the Saints. But to a Hindu, our saints look very like the secondary gods in his Pantheon. The saints play an enormous rôle in the Christianity of the thirteenth and fourteenth centuries; the Christian born here in Verrières felt a very close and particular link with the saint of Verrières. As for the prophets . . . the prophet is not a saint. People have gone to the trouble of hunting through the Old Testament for passages from the prophets that anticipate the essential texts of the Gospels, including the very greatest of all: 'God is Love'. And they have found them, but the context is never quite right. 'God is Love' is there all right, but you don't find: 'love your neighbour as yourself, for my sake'; there is always a dimension lacking; the prophet is clearly speaking for Israel, but he seems to be talking to himself, to be delivering a sort of improvised, panic-stricken soliloquy . . . You never feel in any of them what is so clear in St. Francis of Assisi: 'I say to all those about me: my sister the rain, and they will have a relationship with the rain that they never had before . . .' That you don't find . . . The prophets, at best, are saying: 'Those who listen to me will have a relationship with God that they ought never to have lost, and which they are culpable for having lost. I will restore God to them.' That you do find. But only God. God but not the rain. However, you were talking about Job."

"Yes, *Job*. One of the most extraordinary books in the Old Testament, the one that records the most shocking dialogue man has ever had with his God. A dialogue crammed with meaning and anguish, in which the Jewish interrogation of the universe reaches an intensity rarely found in the Bible. The only thing I can think of as a possible rival to it is Abraham offering up Isaac as a sacrifice to Yahveh."

"Jewish, you say. That remains to be seen . . . There are experts arguing about that at the moment. Some of them say that *Job* is not of Hebrew origin at all, that it is in fact Arabic, in the sense, of course, that it is a product of pre-Islamic Arab culture. They don't dispute the date assigned to it at present, but they do say (and it is curious, it must be admitted . . .) that the book of Job creates a sort of hiatus in the Old Testament, that Job's dialogue with the Eternal is without precedent and without sequel. Perhaps their theory will be ruled out eventually, but it's an interesting one. However, you asked me what connection I see between Job and Prometheus, how they compare. Well, I think that the author of *Job* posits the existence of God, and that

Front page of *L'Indochine enchaînée*, founded and directed by André Malraux

L'Indochine enchaînée

Sommaire

EDITION PROVISOIRE DE L'INDOCHINE PARAISSANT DEUX FOIS PAR SEMAINE, LE MERCREDI ET LE SEMEDI, EN ATTENDANT QUE L'ADMINISTRATION NOUS RENDE OU SE DECIDE A METTRE EN VENTE, LES CARACTERES E'IMPRIMERIE QUI NOUS APPARTIENNENT ET QU'ELLE A CONFISQUES AU MEPRIS DE TOUTE LOI ET DE TOUT USAGE.

DIRECTEURS :

ANDRE MALRAUX ET PAUL MONIN

DIRECTION : 12, RUE TABERD
LE NUMERO ; 20 CENTS.

Editorial

LETTRE OUVERTE A MONSIEUR
ALEXANDRE VARENNE
GOUVERNEUR GENERAL.

Monsieur le Gouverneur Général,

La dé à he annonçant votre nomination au poste que vous allez occuper était à peine parvenue en Cochinchine, que le Gouverneur se mettait à l'œuvre pour vous donner en spectacle, lors de votre arri é., la Comédie qu'on appelle votre Réception

Vous n'é es pas sans avoir entendu parler du mécontentement qui, de jour en jour, grandit en Cochinchine. Vous l'avez marqué dans vos discours, où vous avez parlé, à plusieurs reprises, de réformes nécessaires. Or, il va de soi que lorsque les institutions sont bonnes, il n'est point nécessaire de les réformer ; lorsque les hommes qui les appliquent sont justes, il n'est point nécessaire de les mettre à la retraite.

Donc, vous ne croyiez point que tout allât pour le mieux en Cochinchine. Cette pensée qui annonçait des demandes d'explications, voire même des enquêtes, ne pouvait être admise. Il convenait de vous préparer une Cochinchine toute en or, avec de beaux discours dans lesquels l'émotion voilât l'indigence de la lan ue française ; de vous faire savoir que le Gouverneur Cognacq est aimé de ses administrés ; de former un bloc impressionnant et de vous amener, enfin, à vous pénétrer de cette idée que la politique antillaise des pourboires ingénieusement distribués est la plus précieuse acquisition de l'esprit français et la base de toute action coloniale.

Maintenant, Monsieur le Gouverneur général, que les diverses fanfares vous laissent en paix, nous voudrions vous demander un effort : celui de lire cette lettre, dans laquelle nous avons l'intention d'établir ceci :

Front page of L'Indochine Enchaînée, *November 18, 1925.*

the author of *Prometheus* doesn't. What is Zeus? A tyrant, clearly. But apart from that . . ."

"But Job's God is also a tyrant?"

"The genius of *Job* is that it says for the first time: 'Poor fool, by what right have you started to believe that you can think me? . . . I am God, and forever in-accessible, and my designs are impenetrable . . .' In short, it seems to come from the abyss, it is a proclama-tion of the holy as utterly-other . . . . That absolute-otherness being supreme power . . . It is the greatest dialogue that exists between God and man. If you had to write a piece about Prometheus, I don't mean the masterpiece but the myth itself, then you'd be forced to say: 'It is a conflict between two characters; one of them, Prometheus, I can understand well enough, I can write a dozen paragraphs developing his rôle, quoting what he says . . . But what about the other, Zeus? He just runs through your fingers like water . . .'"

"Do you think of Isaiah's presentiments as valid?"

"The double meaning of presentiment in French is interesting, because double meanings are never a product of chance. When we say *pressentir*, we can mean to predict, or we can mean 'to find out what someone else is thinking'. The prophet is at the same time the man who speaks what God is thinking and the man who predicts the future. The two things aren't completely separate though, because the man who speaks in God's name is also, to some degree, the possessor of the future. The great prophetic spirits aren't clairvoyants, but they have nevertheless achieved a victory over what we call history, and also, more tritely, over the present."

"What do you think of St. John of the Cross, that silent and obscure saint . . ."

"Why St. John of the Cross? He wasn't particularly silent, and he was rather suspect too."

"Suspect?"

"He only just avoided excommunication. When St. Teresa asked for communion and was refused, it was St. John who brought it to her. Legend or history? Even the legend would be significant . . .

"But your idea is more important than that. A silent, obscure saint, why not? But in that case he should be really silent, really obscure, not St. John of the Cross, a saint whose life on earth has left so little trace that neither you nor I even know his name. Why not? But I'd

André Malraux around the
time of *La Condition
humaine*

like to know what a priest would have to say about it. Because an unknown saint is almost inevitably a saint without fellow men, without a neighbor. In a neighbor's eyes it would be difficult for him to be so very obscure. We don't have to define the saint by his works, but can we do without a neighbor? That's much more important than the works. I'm no expert on theological questions, but I think that's where the idea would break down. What you are postulating, briefly, is one of the faithful being sanctified solely by the depth and quality of his love, his love of God. Wouldn't the court (what's it called? . . . The court of beatification, I think) reply that a Christian saint has to be a saint with a neighbour?"

He seemed to be thinking out loud, following some inner argument with himself suddenly, visibly pursuing for the space of a lightning flash that perpetually renewed, tirelessly probing meditation so characteristic of the man. For an instant I was given the revelation of an unwearying, resolutely lucid quest. Pascal was not so far away . . . The nobility of doubt.

"Is there a primacy of contemplation over action?"

"I think that's just a play on words. Obviously one needs to contemplate in order to act, and act in order to contemplate. Thirty years ago I said something like: to transmute as wide an experience as possible into conscious thought."

"Do you still maintain the same position in relation to Christianity that you expressed in *The Temptation of the West*?"

"It wasn't a total position."

"What face does Christ have for you today?"

"None. Either through his biography or through his words, all-important though they are. The supposedly historic character of Christ, I mean — disregarding for the moment the notion of incarnation — the character we meet in the Gospels, consists of momentous words, it isn't a character as such. I'm almost prepared to say, as Gide rather devilishly did, that the proof he was Christ is what he said. The vast iconography, with which I am familiar enough in all conscience, brings me nothing, except its poetry. And yet there is something fascinating about the biographical element that Christianity offers instead of Olympus. I mean that Christ was born in specifically determined circumstances: there is the manger, there are the Innocents. There is a childhood, with the doctors in the temple. There are all the incidents on which Christianity is based. There is

49

nothing like that with the classical gods: Aphrodite never married, and where was Pluto born? It was Christianity that invented the idea of introducing biography into divinity, from the incarnation through to the crucifixion. And yet that biography, made up of tremendously moving incidents, has no continuity. Just as Christ's teachings have nothing in common with any sort of system. As for reducing those teachings to a series of commandments (something the nineteenth century, among others, did with unashamed abandon), that is simply to replace a religion with a moral code. And any truly religious person will tell you how horrifying he finds that. The priest here in Verrières, a former worker-priest I believe, once told me that he considers it the ultimate scandal that religion could ever be confused with a moral code. If you are a believing Christian, then Christ is a person to the very highest degree. If you are an agnostic, then he is not a person at all. The paintings of the highest genius inspired by Catholicism are hypotheses, those inspired by Byzantine Christianity are symbols."

"You have spoken of the spirit of evil. What do you mean by that? The devil is the force that drives man to destroy himself, you said. How great a margin of liberty do we have?"

"On the subject of Evil with a capital E, one must be very careful, because all our really big words — Evil, Love, God — are in fact domains made up of overlapping ideas. God means creator, love, unity, etc. etc. This isn't just a matter of chance, it is because the key-words around which we order our thoughts don't express single ideas, they express domains of ideas and feelings. Evil is one of those domains. It must inevitably evade our definitions. We can always say: it is the opposite of good, then work our way through all Plato's passages on 'the good' again — an effort well worth the trouble, of course — but we are still no further forward. Every time we try to pin down the definition of any domain it will disappear; a definition explosive enough in its effect will last fifty years, perhaps a century, but after that it will fade away. In fact it might be very interesting to isolate the concept of evil inherent in representative texts at three hundred year intervals and compare them. Say in 1700, 1400, then 1100: it's not the same Satan, it isn't even the same Evil."

"Leaving aside the margin of liberty question, what is your attitude to sacrifice? Could you clarify your conception of it?"

"On the subject of sacrifice I must return to my word domain. For me, sacrifice is the only domain with a strength equal to that of Evil — as the Crucifixion

André Malraux in Indochina

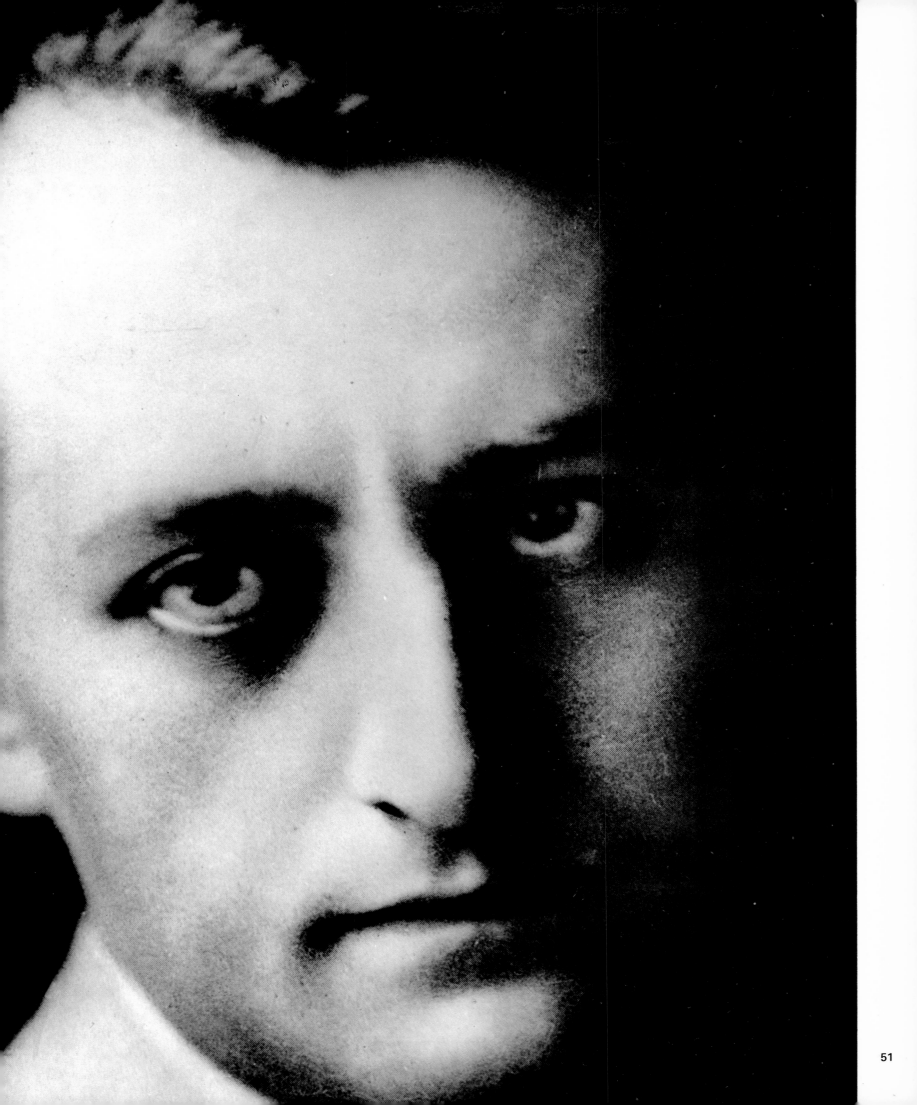

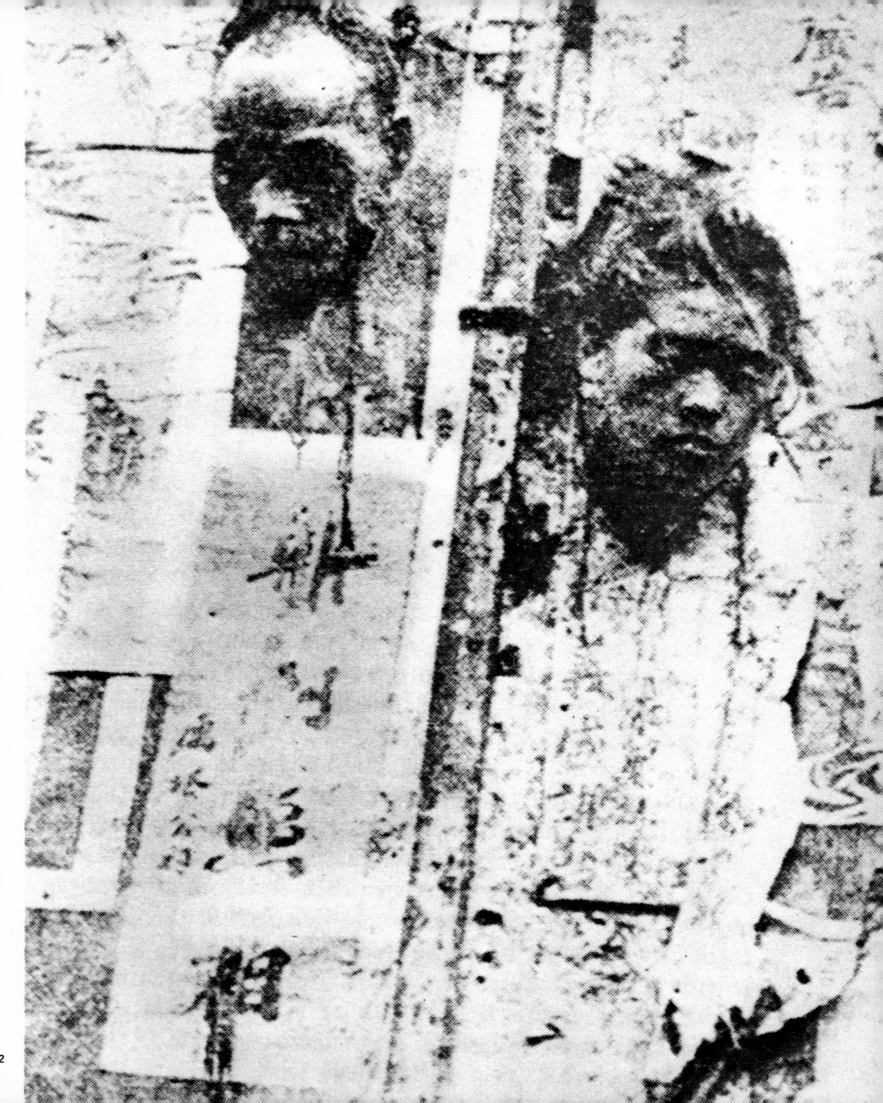

< *La Condition humaine*
(1933)

Jacket design of the
Yiddish translation of
La Condition humaine (1935)

admirably demonstrates, since Christianity is an answer to metaphysical Evil, and its answer is the crucifixion."

"Then could you clarify your conception of transcendence. If there is a transcendence, is there not also a trans-ascendence and a trans-descendence?"

"I term transcendence that part of the unknown to which we refer ourselves. There are a great many unknowns, but there are some unknowns to which we don't refer ourselves, and we refer ourselves to many things that are not unknown. If you have the time, think of all the unknowns to which we do refer ourselves: the list begins with death and ends with God. And the domain they share is that of transcendence."

"What is your position with regard to the transcendent values of pity and charity?"

"That rather brings us back to what we have just been saying about the crucifixion. Dostoievsky's is one famous answer: the total rejection of a world in which 'the torture of one innocent child by a brute can exist'. Beyond doubt, charity — and you mean charity in the sense of love, of course — beyond doubt, charity is a certain domain of mystery. I wrote once, and I was including pity and charity, that Evil is the profoundest accusation that exists. And yet the torture of an innocent child by a brute has no greater importance, in that essential domain where Dostoievsky takes his stand, than any particular act of heroism or love. And perhaps of pity and charity. Sacrifice is without doubt one pole of the irrational, the irrationality of evil being the other."

"Could one, on just this plane, establish a parallel between Rembrandt and Rouault?"

"None whatever. Rembrandt's crucial achievement was discovering in light, the physical lighting he employed, a source of emotion. His light is not a luminous light, it is light converted into emotive power. Take his *Christ at Emmaus*: it is immediately obvious that the light and shade he uses play the same rôles as the right and left hands on a keyboard. He hasn't just decided to have a light source at such and such a point, with darkness beyond it, he is inventing a technique for suggesting divinity, the presence of Christ, similar to that available to music. A method without which he wouldn't be Rembrandt. It's a problem that doesn't exist for Rouault. Light in his work plays a completely different rôle: he is trying to paint the icons of modern art. The Byzantines had grasped perfectly that you couldn't paint a portrait of Christ. Rembrandt tried it nineteen times, I believe. He never succeeded except

<André Malraux and Sergei
Mikhailovitch Eisenstein
working on the filmscript of
La Condition humaine (1934)

André Malraux in 1928, the
year of *Les Conquérants*

when there were other characters present: in his
Christ at Emmaus and *The Tribute Money*. But he tried
the single portrait seventeen times, which means that
sixteen times he had to try again. El Greco alone
succeeded with what Rembrandt was trying to do,
because he remembered the icons. The icon can
represent Christ because it is not the representation of a
man, it is a symbol. Of course it is an affective sign, a
sign working directly through the senses, as you wish,
but it is a sign. What Rouault attempted, though using
methods that owe nothing to Byzantium, was of the
order of the icon, whereas Rembrandt was hoping to
achieve direct suggestion of the sacred, the divine, by a
lyrical use of light and shadow. And I happen to believe
that no one has successfully suggested holiness except
in the fields of the icon and Gregorian chant. Even with
Beethoven there's something that isn't quite right.
Praise of Christ is not a reflection of Christ. The theo-
logians say that they term 'sacred' that which belongs to
God as God. As soon as human genius deserted
symbolic means and turned to direct representation, or
emotional means in music, the sacred vanished from
art."

"Don't you think we might say though, looking at
Rembrandt, that there is an art of pity and charity?"

"In that context I would be more inclined to think of
painting from the time of St. Francis through to Fra
Angelico, and Fra Angelico wasn't a Franciscan. There
I do see an art of pity — or compassion perhaps? As for
Rembrandt, compare Angelico's most moving work
with the *Christ at Emmaus*: the disparity is apparent at
once. The great Christian art of pity and charity exists.
It is the Christ in Chartres (the one in the transept),
Giotto, Tuscan and Umbrian art up to Fra Angelico, and
to a large degree also, Gothic art up to the death of St.
Louis."

"As we talked just now about the Old Testament, it
came to me that you have never visited either the Negev
or Jerusalem. The reason I thought of the Negev is that
its name in Hebrew has a very precise meaning, that of
void, nothingness — *La Nada*. Jerusalem is the embodiment of a presence, which we can address either by the
name of Yahveh or by the name of Christ. Yet somehow
it seems to me that if you have never been to the Negev,
the reason is that you are there. Am I wrong?"

"I have no idea, I don't think so. As far as Jerusalem
is concerned, you will find the explanation in the
memoirs my friend the Abbé Bockel[1] has just had

[1] Pierre Bockel, *L'Enfant du rire*; Preface by André Malraux. Paris 1973.

59

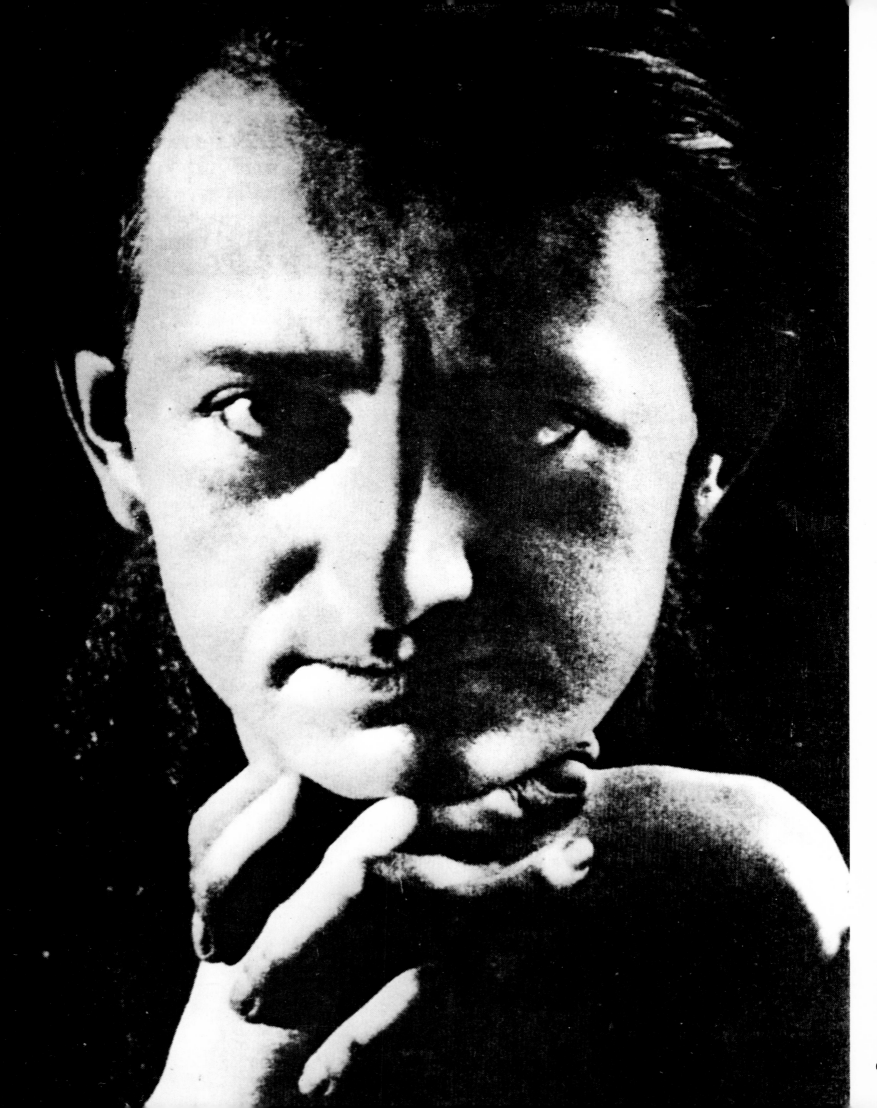

published. I went seven times to Asia, from the coast to Persia or India overland. I never went to Jerusalem. I have no Christian faith whatever, but I don't feel that Jerusalem ought to be a mere tourist attraction. The idea of people sightseeing in Gethsemane fills me with horror."

"Various civilizations have summoned you, as it were, and you have tried to answer their summonses, to elucidate their messages. India, for instance, cast a spell over you. Jerusalem does not possess any specific art of its own, or any monuments capable of attracting you perhaps, yet it does radiate a very particular light of its own. It is the crucible of Christian art, the embodiment of a myth. Yet you seem to have kept away from it quite deliberately."

"What keeps me away from Jerusalem is the garden on the Mount of Olives. Either you go to Jerusalem as a pilgrim or you don't go at all. If you are a Christian, then you go, and bravo! In the Middle Ages, as you know, when you had committed murder you were sent on a pilgrimage to Jerusalem, and generally you didn't come back. Which seems to me absolutely fitting. But as an attraction for the merely curious . . .

"As for my connection with India, that's something different. I was formed by Christianity, I was a believing Christian until the age of sixteen, Christianity has a reality for me that Buddhism, however much I may know about it, cannot attain; I have never been a Buddhist. Secondly, there is something unique in Christianity, something you asked me about earlier: sacrifice. I don't wish to go sightseeing in Gethsemane, but I have been to Assisi. The garden where St. Francis talked to the birds is not the same as Calvary. If you are a believer, so much the better, but if you aren't, then it's still very lovely all the same. Sarnath is the place where Buddha preached before the gazelles (he was preaching to the disciples who had first abandoned him, then returned, but the gazelles listened). The fact that there is so little grass in India makes the emotional effect of Sarnath's great expanse of turf even greater. There are still gazelles, and the whole park has a most unusual poetic quality. Christ's garden is another thing altogether. But I am not trying to put myself in the right, I am only trying to answer your question."

"Let's go back to the subject of action and try to define it."

"Action, like Evil, is a domain. Don't think I'm trying to evade the problem: in my eyes that is a fundamental fact. The only way to think a domain is by feeling your way around it, as it were. Its total meaning comes from the superimposed meanings of which it is com-

< Manuscript of *Les Conquérants*

< During the year (1930) of *La Voie royale*

With Maxim Gorky (1934)

62

posed. As soon as you start peeling them away you kill your quarry."

"Is the adventure of action a product of adventure of the mind, each reciprocally inspiring the other?"

"Such coincidence is rare, I would say; there is no great reason why it should be so, but that's how it is. Men of action are rarely intellectuals, and intellectual or spiritual people are rarely capable of action. We are back in some degree to your previous question. Why shouldn't contemplation lead on to nobler action, and action to deeper contemplation? It almost never happens. There is no example of an Aristotle who was an Alexander, no example of an Alexander who was an Aristotle."

"True. In your own case, though, I do believe that your life, and of course your work, which is the expression of it, correspond to a perpetual dialectic, leading you from thought to action, then back again. Action nourishing thought which is then expressed in further action."

"With me there is a rather curious point of intersection that you might call 'poetry' — the word is somewhat slight — perhaps 'the imaginary' would be better . . ."

"The poem?"

"But if we were to go on to men of really first importance, then that wouldn't hold good any more. And yet even Alexander was haunted by a need to exist in an imaginary way that belongs in the realm of poetry . . . When he thought he was doomed to die of thirst in the desert, he said: 'Athenians, what must a man not do to earn your praise!' He went to the oasis of Ammon in order to be told that he was the son of Zeus or the serpent . . . Despite everything though, however prodigious the poem he bequeathed to us, Alexander didn't write it."

"I must have been sixteen when I read *La Condition humaine* for the first time. You were already a myth for me. You expressed the archetypes that emerge at that very precisely circumscribed moment in life we call adolescence. At the time, I thought of you as fulfilling that rôle for me alone, though of course I realized later that you had ultimately fulfilled it for an entire generation, the one now at its noon. You know that marvellous Miloscz poem *Nihumin*: 'Forty years, forty years, learning how to love and how to suffer . . .' If we could have done again what Malraux did. Rediscover that agonizing harmony between thought and action. It is

Clara, Malraux's first wife

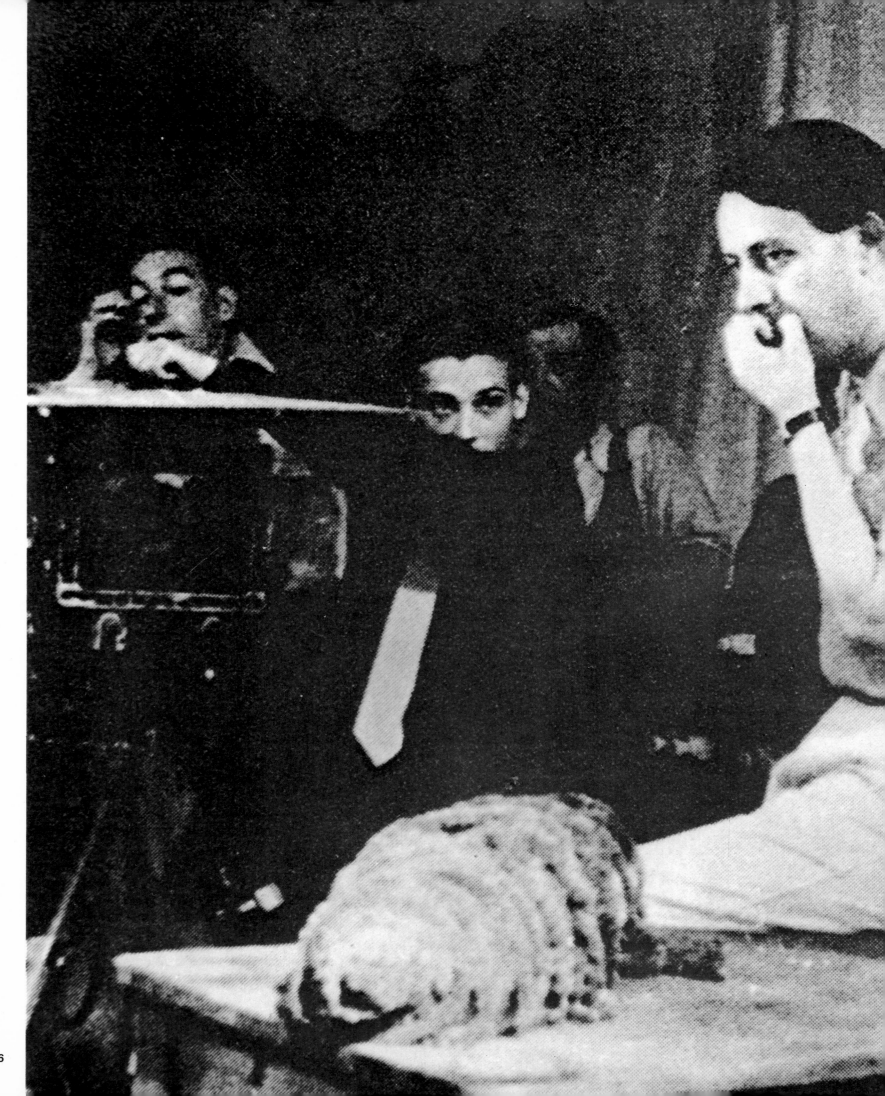

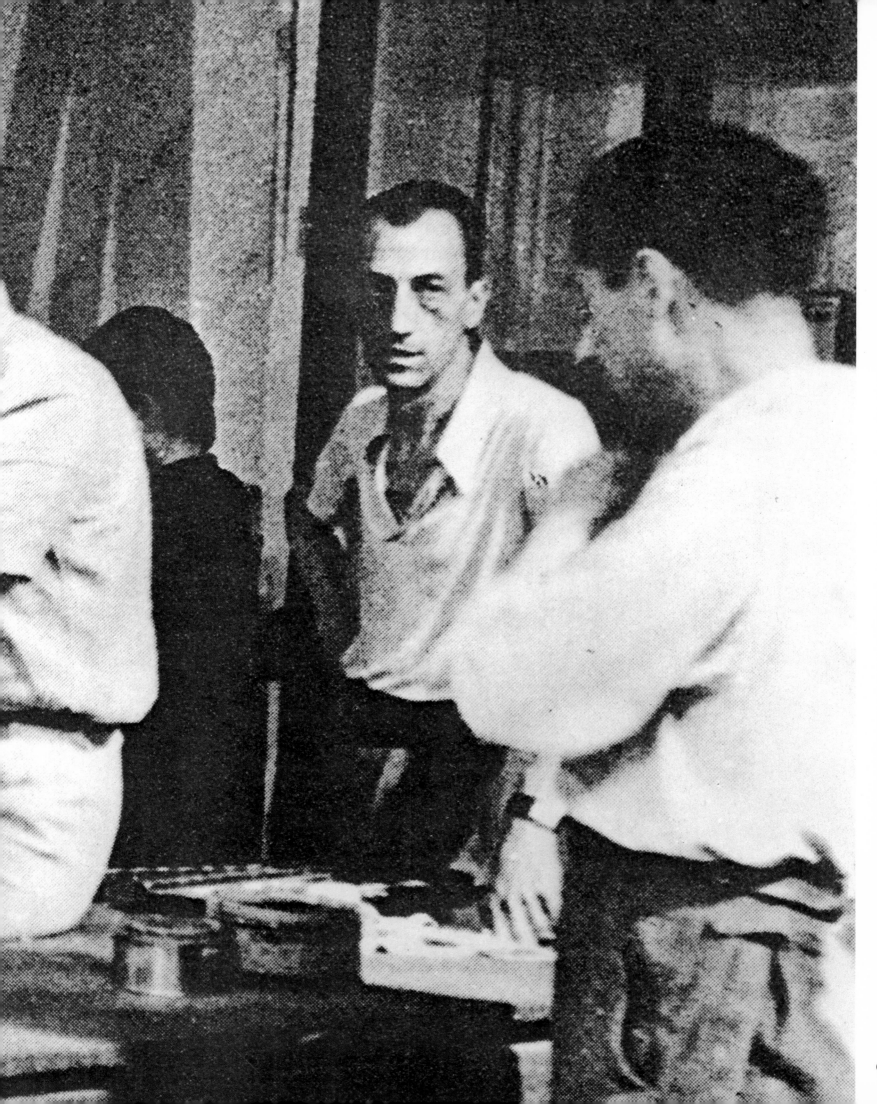

that balance, that harmony in your life that so staggers me."

"There is something rather similar in the great Romantics. Though it's curious that I should have been a successor to the anti-Romantic reaction, to symbolism. Baudelaire and Rimbaud became archetypes by following other paths, but Lamartine was President of the Republic. If he had died in 1848, as the revolutionary leader . . . There's something of the same thing in Byron. He was in fact the prototype of the great French Romantics in that field. Think of Victor Hugo in exile on Guernsey and dreaming of dying at Missolonghi . . ."

"Do you feel today that your thought and your action are slipping away from you; that you are no longer able to view either of them other than isolated from you by what Brecht, with reference to the actor, called an 'alienation effect'?"

"All that is for others now. It must of necessity slip away from me. As Valéry says, once you have seen a number of schools flourish and die, you come to realize that any work, and even more so any life, undergoes a metamorphosis. I know what *La Condition humaine* was when the book was first published. It is quite certain that you read it as something else. I should like to analyze the strange life of their own that works carry within themselves. After fifty years you have neither the same past nor the same future, because the future of your predecessors is your present. But time is only part of the metamorphosis."

"We are back with the transcendence we were talking about just now."

"It could always be called that, since you are right about the works. And if there is some part of a man's life more or less bound up with a dream, that too is probably transformed in the same way as a work: Lawrence of Arabia as well as *Le Cid*."

"Could you have found yourself on the other side?"

"What do you mean by the other side? Fascism? Or something else?"

"In the name of what did you choose justice, dignity, freedom? Why didn't you put yourself first? Why didn't you put style before values?"

"I think that Indochina played an all-important rôle in my life. When the Indochinese defended me, something shifted inside. Not that I was on some other

68

side before. The other side was just indifference. But the bond with, well, it's a simplification but let's say social justice, was born at that moment. But do we really know whether the crucial actions of any life are the product of a choice, or whether what seems to be choice is only rationalization? But that's enough about that. You asked why I chose as I did. It isn't of much interest to me. You've read that thing of Claudel's: 'This puppet I lug about in front of me by the name of Paul Claudel . . .' I feel rather like that too. There are those who feel quite differently, and with equal justification. As for style and values, it seems to me that in that domain we are summoned. I am not ignorant of music, but there is simply no comparison. I know the art galleries of Europe picture by picture, whereas I love music merely as an amateur who has listened to a great many records, from Perrotin to Varèse; the two things are different in kind. And it isn't because I made the choice. I love music very much. It is because I was bewitched . . . the word is excessive, and yet . . . My literary education, on the other hand, let's say that was cubist: Apollinaire, Max Jacob, etc., and my taste for the great French Romantics at the same time, that was something very rare in those days. I can remember defending Victor Hugo against all comers during the heyday of the *Nouvelle Revue Française* group. Claudel used to speak very unkindly indeed about Hugo in those days, Gide thought I admired *Olympio* for sentimental, nostalgic reasons, and so on, Paulhan thought I was mad, Arland sat on the fence, and Supervielle too. Literature began with Rimbaud, or let's say Baudelaire; to admire the great Romantics was downright criminal, let them stay in limbo where they belonged! And another writer I admired, though he too rated less than nothing at the N.R.F., was Chateaubriand, the Chateaubriand of the *Mémoires*, needless to say."

"Claudel came under his spell a little toward the end."

"The spell of what? The style?"

"The style, and a certain inspiration after all."

"Claudel wasn't exclusively a man of letters; he was one to a certain degree, but privately, and besides that wasn't really an essential characteristic; whereas it's easy to see that the measure of Gide's veneration for Baudelaire was also the measure of his loathing for Chateaubriand."

I noticed that the crown of rainsoaked trees in the distance was being lit up by the already westering sun. Darkness was creeping into the room where we sat,

André Malraux

and the face of the speaker opposite me was standing out more and more from its background, highlighted by the strange parasol. The things all around us seemed to be waiting without impatience for our dialogue to be over, so that they could resume their own soliloquies.

"There are two peoples that constitute a great reservoir of humanity in Europe, Spain and Russia, both of which have their Canto Hondo: two peoples, two dictatorships. How is it that their two great impulses towards freedom, their two attempts at absolute democracy, have resulted in such a devaluation of human quality?"

"When you say attempts at absolute democracy clearly you mean the *Frente Popular*, not Franco. Well now, in Russia the Revolution triumphed. In Spain it was defeated. But that's not the crux of your question. With Russia, I think the answer hinges to a fairly large degree on the legacy of Byzantium — the Byzantium that the Russians will tell you had at least one empress every hundred years who killed or blinded her husband or her children. St. Louis would not have been at all pleased about such behavior. He would have thumped on the table and said: faith, yes, faith is all very well, but a Christian must also be responsible for his actions. In the nineteenth century, that responsibility became its own caricature: a moral code. In Byzantium, if you died in union with Christ it didn't matter all that much what you had done before. There is no moral indignation in Byzantine history. And you find the legacy of that in Dostoievsky. His notebooks for *The Idiot* reveal the evolution of that sublime final scene: Myshkin and Rogojine keeping vigil over the dead Nastasia. In the first version, the murderer was Myshkin; in other words, the literary character closest to Christ. Stalin used to say: 'Russians are part Spartan, part Byzantine; the Spartan part is good.' I was in Russia in 1934, I missed all but the very beginning of the purges . . ."

"You were there before Gide?"

"Yes. I came away two months after the murder of Kirov, which triggered off the whole thing. During those two months the feeling was: what's happening? Ultimately, it was: right, Stalin's made up his mind; he may be right and he may be wrong, but he's Stalin. Some people assume nowadays that he had Kirov killed, but at that time the thought just didn't occur. It was in order to avenge Kirov that he unleashed the purges. At all events, if I am to sum up my feeling about Russia, then I am bound to say that even during its darkest days I found a humanity there that would fare badly if judged by St. Louis, but rather well judged

Speaking for Spain in the
U.S. (1938)

A shot from the film
Sierra de Teruel, based on
L'Espoir >

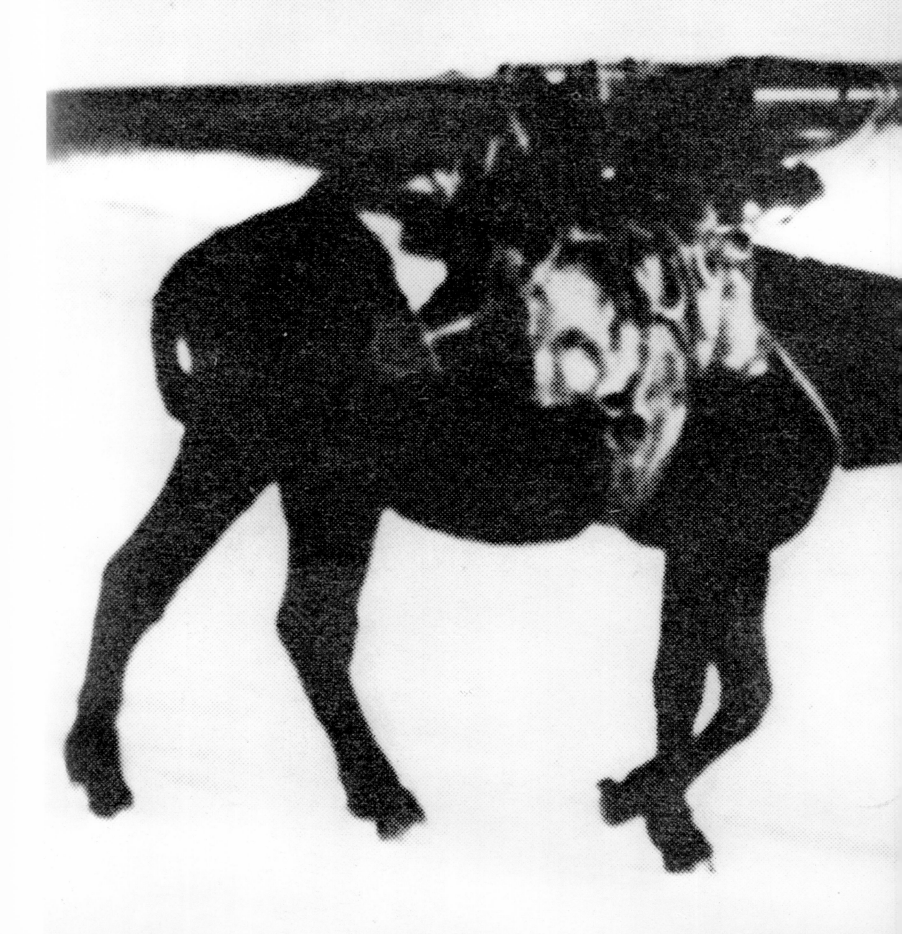

according to Dostoievsky, a humanity that moreover displayed one of the profoundest senses of fraternity in Europe."

"When the Spanish Civil War broke out, Spain had just rediscovered its 'Deep Song'. It was being wakened out of a long lethargy (disregarding Unamuno in the nineteenth century) by the voices of Lorca, Alberti, Machado, and later on Neruda. Franco's regime seems to be draining its life blood."

"Bergamín should be on that list too. I wonder whether any country that has recently been bled in that way is not bound to go through a period of convalescence . . . Almost all those you mentioned live outside Spain now; they have no successors, that's certain. But here, after the Revolution, how long did it take France to rediscover true literature? And besides, Spanish literature has never had the continuity of French or English literature. There was no successor to *Don Quixote* either. It is a literature (and this is true of their painting too, I might add) that tends to progress in a series of lightning flashes; between Velasquez and Goya there is just a black hole."

"A succession of dazzling Renaissances."

"The fascination of the Renaissance for us is its colossal productivity, something that hasn't happened again since. If we didn't know that a man named Shakespeare did actually exist, we would say that his work was a collective effort. If we didn't have a biography for Rabelais, we would say that Pantagruel was a collective work; that verbal frenzy, beside which Céline is just a schoolboy, suggests a synthesis of selected invective from at least fifteen prodigiously gifted cab drivers . . . After the Elizabethans the torrent dwindled, after Rabelais too, and similarly after the masters of the Siglo de Oro in Spain."

"The generation of Spanish writers I listed just now, could they have created a new Siglo de Oro?"

"No, no! They certainly represent an important expression of Spain, they are certainly great talents, but for me the Siglo de Oro is something altogether different. I never think of the writers of Spain's Golden Age as writers, in the same way as you never think of Shakespeare as a writer. You know that he turned out plays, you may perhaps have directed some of them! But you don't think of him as you think of . . . even of Claudel, and yet Claudel wasn't just a man of letters. You've seen Claudel sitting down at his desk to, how did he phrase it? — to put some starch into an act; you can't imagine Shakespeare like that."

Spain, 1936

André Malraux in Spain.
Right, Max Aub, designer of
Sierra de Teruel (1938) >

76

"Claudel wrote for an hour a day."

"But every day, that's a lot!"

"The rest of the time he was dealing with his mail."

"Yes, his mail . . . He used to write the answers in the margins."

He smiled for the first time. A mischievous, conspiratorial smile, full of humor. But the moment of relaxation was brief, then he was clearly waiting for my next serve.

"What are politics? The Old Testament gives us a fairly precise definition: the pursuit of justice. Do you accept that?"

"The pursuit of justice is doubtless one of the good definitions, but it isn't the only one. For me, politics have never existed. What does exist is history. I found myself in politics because it is the medium of history, and there is no other. But a politics without history is also without interest. The day General de Gaulle announced his resignation I made it clear that I was also handing in mine, and I haven't set foot in a council since the government was dissolved. My political activity has always been bound up with the Revolution, then the Nation, the Resistance, and General de Gaulle; politics I know nothing about. However, since you are taking the word in its general, quasi-historical meaning, then I will say this: apart from the will to justice, there is also another element we mentioned very briefly earlier, something that you might term the romance of history. A will to participate in history is also, after all, a will to belong to mankind, to nations, to privileged moments, in a domain that is not solely that of reality, one that we are forced to call, for want of anything better, the realm of legend. You feel it very strongly with Napoleon; there is no possible doubt that he was consciously competing with Plutarch's Great Men. In the Convention, it's impossible to miss it. Remember Saint-Just, leaping up onto the rostrum and yelling: 'The world has been empty since the Romans!' No conception of historical action is possible if you suppress that element. It's a pretty variable one; however, even in countries where today's history is of crucial importance, like China, you still find that men are under the spell of their heroic or glorious past. When I asked Mao: 'Don't you think of yourself as the successor of the Great Emperors?', he answered: 'But of course!' And he is a revolutionary. In India, on the other hand, which hasn't had any historical heroes (though it has had conquerors or unifiers), the same thing isn't true. India dreams of the *Ramayana*, not of Akbar, not of Asoka. But with us . . . Think of the

In the sky over Spain

weight of Plutarch on European thought! What would Western history be with Plutarch excised? The Graeco-Roman myth filled the whole of Europe, and is still present by proxy. There is no Cato today, but there is Jaurès: the Great Men."

"How do you explain the success of Marxist ideology among so many young French intellectuals when it has failed in Europe as a system of government?"

"Partly by what Marx has to offer those who have really read him — and not him alone. Serious Marxist politics is the politics of those who have also read Lenin. Serious Marxist economics is the economics of those who have read their Ricardo. Partly too by the romance of history I have just been talking about. And partly, last of all, quite simply by conformism. The conformism of the present myth of the Left still awaits its novelist. And what makes it all the more interesting is that there is no longer any myth of the Right. And added to those attitudes, there is also another important domain, that of negative emotions. Men have experienced extremely strong collective emotions: the Crusades were a genuine response to 'It is God's will!' There are also negative emotions, and they are no less powerful. In politics, 'the spirit of opposition' really means something. Nine-tenths of our Communist voters actually vote Communist not because they are Marxists but because they think they will make things more difficult for the government than by voting Socialist; if they knew of another left wing party that had the same strength as Communism (and a Soviet Union behind it), then they would vote for that. A negative emotion. This negative emotion with regard to society played a large rôle in May 1968; as it did in the hippy movement when that was at its height. Any analysis of an age ought to weigh its negative emotions against its positive ones. The former are by no means merely the obverse of the latter. And the negative ones never seem to have any really far-reaching effect. I doubt if any significant action is going to emerge from the pseudo-Marxism of today's intelligentsia. Leninism, for example, did not emerge from a negative emotion."

Malraux's knowledge of the work and thought of Jung might have led him to go on and analyze his concept of "negative emotions" more fully. In fact, he said no more on the subject.

"Are aesthetics and ethics interdependent for you?"

"What do we mean by aesthetics? Valéry once said, very reasonably: 'It is, in whole or in part, the technique of establishing a recipe for the infallible manufacture of masterpieces.' In which case, so much the worse for

< André Malraux at the time of his last air missions in Spain (1936)

In the Spanish air force

84

aesthetics. As long as art recognizes norms, everything goes swimmingly; but if it doesn't recognize them, or if they haven't yet been worked out, then things become much more difficult. An aesthetics like that of beauty in the classical era is easy enough to define: it is simply dealing with a process of idealization in painting or in sculpture. But reflection on the painting of Picasso could hardly be called an aesthetics. It is modern art that questions the validity of previous aesthetics, I would say, rather than the other way about. At present, our values in art are empirical. We shall arrive at an intellectual conception of them eventually, of course; but I doubt whether that conception will take the form of an aesthetics. The specific values of art belong in a domain that is no longer that of aesthetics; as for the others, the sacred, violence, they certainly require something more than an aesthetics. Even the word itself is an embarrassment to us."

I was forcibly reminded that the man speaking had for ten years been France's Minister for Cultural Affairs. I was one of his followers in the task of implanting throughout France — with more or less success — those Maisons de Culture that were intended, theoretically, to fling wide their doors to all those previously denied access to the great works of art that are the living witness of our long past and our uncertain present. Jeanne Laurent had been the first to break the ground, immediately after the Liberation, with the creation of the regional Centres Dramatiques. And such was the inspiration behind the project that it did jolt some life at last even into provincial France, that other France, beginning a hundred miles or so from Paris, that still clung to a belief, cherished by its local dignitaries, that the fire-break of a cultural desert could still hold back for years to come what were in fact ineluctable changes. The theatre, painting, art in general, it was still accepted, were all reserved in the first place for Paris alone, which then graciously treated our provincial burghers to the delights of its successes at secondhand, in the form of a few second-rate tours.

André Malraux alone had the power to create such enthusiasm, arouse such commitment, light so many torches. It was through him, with him, that we set out on the only crusade justifiable in our day, that of a perpetually self-questioning freedom. The departure of General de Gaulle and his minister seemed to set the seal of failure upon this great project. But what is done is done. An irreversible process has been set in motion. The fact that it may founder in mediocrity is no concern of his.

I looked into the eyes looking into mine, and I couldn't resist asking:

"What would your definition of culture be?"

< At Chival airport (1936)

At Pontigny, a village and château used as a gathering place for intellectuals

André Malraux, 34-year-old pilot >

90

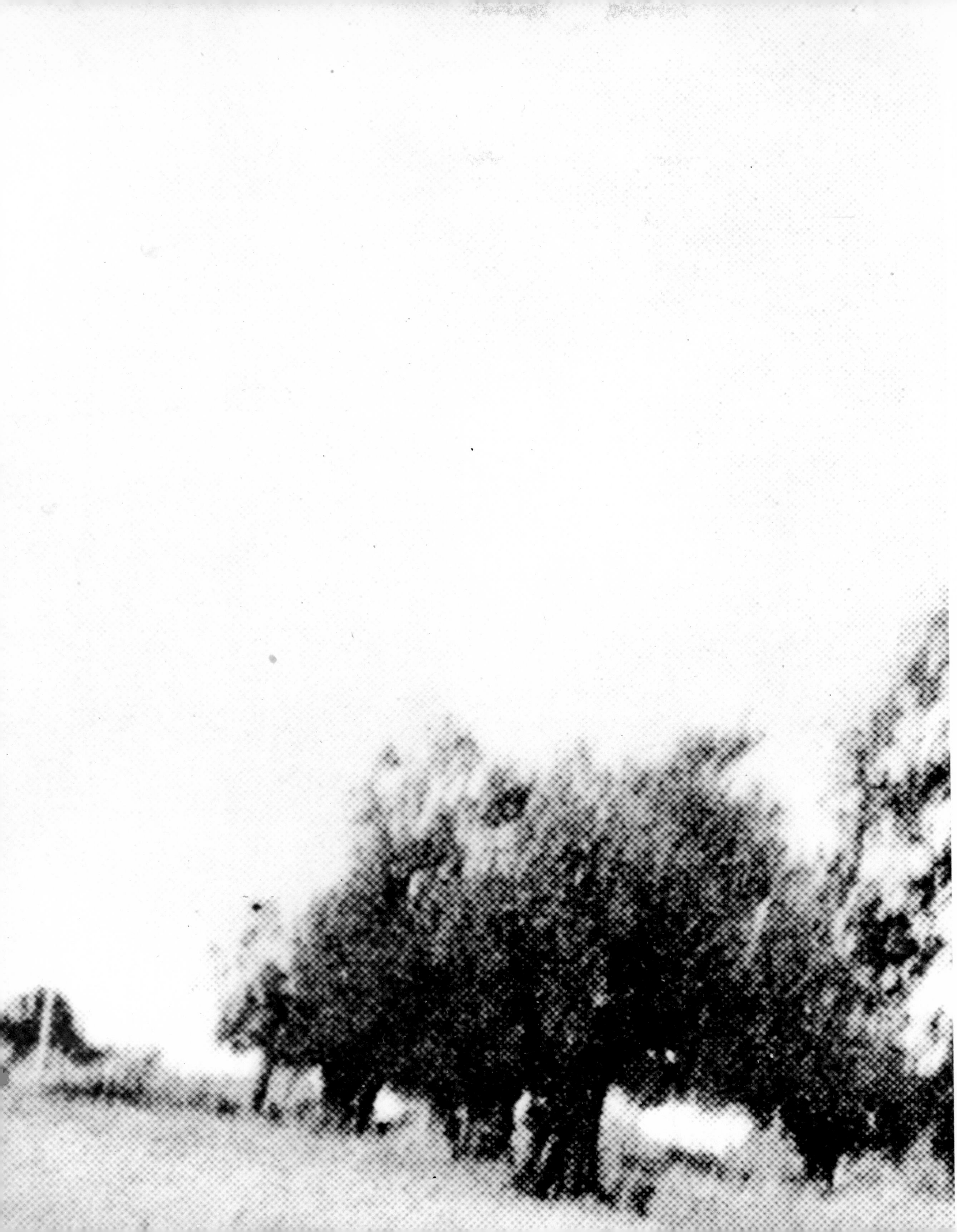

"The one I gave in the Chamber of Deputies was impromptu, though that certainly didn't stop it catching on: knowledge of the greatest number of works by the greatest number of men. I was answering some nitwit or other. More seriously, I wrote earlier, in *Les Voix de Silence*, that culture is the heritage left by the world's nobility. But it's also quite interesting trying to define it by its opposite. I also wrote once — do you remember? — that it is exceedingly hard to define dignity but easy to define humiliation: everyone knows only too well what a slap in the face is like. And it's harder to define culture than to experience its opposite. All culture, quite clearly, entails a referral back to the human quality it recognizes in its dead. Our culture begins with a knowledge of what the greatest minds have thought, the greatest artists created. At one time, we could happily have said: the heritage of truth. But we don't say that today. The highest culture is perhaps nothing but a knowledge of man's noblest dialogues — even in art. It's something I've already written about in the past: 'If the Greek philosophers had met the prophets, what would they have had to exchange, other than insults? Before Plato could meet Christ, Montaigne had to be born.' But for Montaigne's thought to be born, Christ's meeting with Plato had to be possible."

With his last sentence scarcely finished, he stood up and went over to shake hands with the technicians. Then he came back towards me, relaxed, smiling.

"A good first set, I think. Now it's up to you to arrange the rest of the match."

He held out his hand, the hand I had watched constantly darting out from his face into space, accompanying all the varied rhythms of his thought as it searched, settled on its quarry, questioned what it felt it had grasped, and which in the only battle worth the trouble of fighting possessed only one weapon: human dignity.

The parasol had been switched off and evening darkness filled the room. As soon as he was gone, I had an unpleasant feeling of being an intruder. Furniture, paintings, everything in the room was telling me it was time to go. Our tiny team of technicians was dismantling, rewinding, unplugging, and I suddenly felt I was back on one of our decentralization tours, in some provincial assembly rooms with the curtain scarcely down, yet already obliged to strike our set and whisk it off elsewhere.

Malraux emerges from the shadow

It was 1954. Rafael Alberti and José Bergamín had both come on the same evening to a performance in the little Left Bank theatre where my production of Federico García Lorca's *Yerma* had just opened. We strolled for a long while together through the Parisian night. They conjured up their past for me, Federico the magician, and the days when Madrid existed solely in order to fête their youth and talent. Listening to Yerma's tragic litany again, both had been struck with amazement to find how clearly the murdered poet's plainsong had unknowingly prophesied the barrenness with which Spain was to be afflicted.

Several years later I met Bergamín a second time in Madrid, between two exiles, and then again in Paris when I asked him to write a Christmas story for the young audiences of the Comédie de la Loire, of which I was then artistic director. Nor was I unaware of the deep bond of friendship that had linked him to André Malraux ever since the Spanish Civil War. A friendship compounded entirely of reciprocal admiration, respect, and modesty.

My links with Spain made me very much aware of the difference of temperament, though not of sensibility, that could have formed a barrier between the two men. But that was to under-rate the privilege that genius grants to the agnostic, grace to the believer. I felt the need to hear an echo of Malraux's thought, as it were, given back by the heir of Philip II and El Greco. High in the dazzling July sky, the plane carrying me towards Bergamín seemed to hang motionless in blue space. I heard his voice over the telephone, telling me that he would agree to see me and was expecting me. With the Pyrenees scarcely behind us, Castile lay revealed in the sun as it "leapt upward with the strength of its mighty thighs". It was ten o'clock. Grays, ochres, coppery greens burned in the heat. It was on a journey across that same Castilian plain, by rail, that Lorca had conceived the idea of writing *Yerma*. A childless woman in that desert of fire. Alone on that arid earth. Here and there, seemingly at random, a hovel blazed with light and poverty. Oh white walls of Spain! In the distance, already the Sierra de Guadarrama and mourning Madrid. With Toledo and the Escorial keeping jealous vigil over her. Here, at this crossroads of East and West,

the whole tragic sense of life had its great flowering. Here, there is no longer any question of that harmony within the tragic that the Greeks gave us. Instead, distortion and death, questioning and self-questioning. The Absolute to which timeless Spain has bowed its neck, accepted once and for all. El Greco illumines and justifies both these attitudes, both these conceptions of the tragic.

El Greco of the last years, beyond technique, would not have recognized in himself the pupil of Tintoretto or the heir of the icons. Serenity has no place here.

Less than an hour after the plane landed I was already in the Plaza de Oriente, so admirably proportioned, surrounded by its tall, ancient houses with their closed shutters, welcoming you into shady interiors where you are enveloped in coolness and the past.

Bergamín's two small rooms up under the roof were flanked by a beautiful terrace crammed with "masetas de malbones y geranios".

"I lived in a district
of Madrid, with bells,
with clocks, with trees.
From where I lived you could look out
on the dry face of Castile
like a leather sea."

Pablo Neruda's lines came to fresh life in that place. José Bergamín stretched out an arm towards the Escorial, a lonely and impregnable fortress in the distance. His whole being, beneath an appearance of fragility, expressed nobility and strength. In the hot wind blowing on the terrace he looked like Don Quixote about to go down into the Cave of Montesinos. It was impossible to stay up there. We would have to go out and search for a little coolness in the shade of one of the bodegas with which Madrid is crammed, and which in those last days of July were mostly closed. But Don José was at home in the capital. He knew every nook and cranny of that city which is "his" city. Madrid the proud, the authentic and living Madrid, offers him back the same generous image of herself that he has presented to her. The ordinary people of the city know neither the work nor the thought of this hidalgo who

André Malraux at 31, the year of his Prix Goncourt

José Bergamín, Paris, November 1973 >

97

has never ceased, throughout all his exiles, to carry his "Spain of the heart" with him. Yet those same people, by some obscure sounding system, are able to sense the presence of essential truths that have no name and are the very fabric of his life.

"¿ Todavia en Madrid, Don José?"
"¡ Me voy dentro de unos dias, niño!"
"¿ Y adonde irá usted, Don José?"
"¡ A Andalucia. A ver como se porta el mar!"
"¿ Como está usted, Don José?"
"¡ Aqui andámos hijo, aqui andámos! Mas jóven cada dia!"
"¡ Con salud, Don José!"
"¡ Adios hijo! Adios!"[1]

Such brief exchanges, interspersed with bursts of laughter, saw us settled at a table with a bottle of Viña Albina. Our conversation, interrupted by a long siesta during the worst heat of the day, was resumed at about ten that evening and continued through to the small hours.

I have reconstructed our dialogue as we noted it down during that suspended moment in time when the heart of Spain, speaking with the voice of one of its great aristocrats, opened itself to that other heart, beyond the Pyrenees, that had never ceased, in its fraternal difference, to fight the same fight.

"Malraux thinks that he is an agnostic and that you are a believer, which takes my mind back to the passage in *Les Chênes qu'on abat* in which Malraux and General de Gaulle each question the other on that subject, and Malraux says: 'He thinks that according to his lights I am a believing Christian, and I think that according to his lights he isn't.'"

[1]"Still in Madrid, Don José?"
"I'll be gone in a day or two, my boy!"
"And where will you go, Don José?"
"To Andalucia, to see how the sea's getting on!"
"How are you then, Don José?"
"As you see, my boy, as you see! Younger every day!"
"Your health, Don José!"
"God be with you, my son, God be with you!"

André Malraux about to set off with Corniglion Molinier on their expedition to find the Queen of Sheba's city in the Yemen

"Exactly. I say that I believe I am a believer. Malraux simply says that he *is* an agnostic. I think for my part, like the General, that Malraux's 'I am an agnostic' also presupposes that he believes he is an agnostic, just as I believe I am a believer. Which would mean, in short, that we are neither of us even sure of being either the one or the other. Which means that we doubt: he that he is an agnostic, myself that I am a believer. Charles Nodier, in a fine story of his, quotes a Spanish proverb: 'De las cosas mas seguras, lo mas seguro es dudar' (Of all certain things the most certain is doubt). Doubts are what provide the believer's nourishment. The man who doesn't believe doesn't doubt. The man who believes doubts. De Gaulle asked Malraux if he was certain of his agnosticism and not of his scepticism. One has the impression, reading Malraux, that he is all the more certain of his agnosticism because, out of sincerity and even out of modesty, he does not dare to conceive of himself as a believer. Which doesn't mean that he eliminates the possibility of becoming one. But to my mind one always senses a certain conscious recalcitrance with Malraux: he *does not wish to believe*. And that, for me, is the best situation in which to find faith. That said, I don't in fact think that one does find faith, but that faith finds us. In a paradoxical way, I would venture to say that it is not we who believe in God but God who believes in us. Which is why I think that revelation and faith are one and the same thing."

"Isn't that Pascal's wager?"

"Clearly it is Pascal. But it is also Nietzsche. A little while ago I published a short book[1] on the sacraments, for which Malraux was kind enough to write a preface displaying his usual acuity and clearsightedness, and I was criticized, when the book came out, for being excessively Spanish in my Catholicism. And yet to me the book is Pascalian. Perhaps I hispanify Pascal. Unless it is Pascal who has hispanified me. Because if I look into the living springs of my Catholic Christianity, I see before all and above all Pascal. And I would

André Malraux

[1]José Bergamín, *Le Clou brûlant*, preface by André Malraux, Paris 1973.

venture to add Nietzsche. Those two, more than the Spanish mystics and Unamuno, and even than Dostoievsky."

"Where Christianity is concerned, Dostoievsky is still always an essential reference point for Malraux, who sees profound spiritual affinities between Spain and Russia. What are your thoughts on that subject?"

"I am in agreement on both points. However, I think we would have to stress the profound differences that divide Russian Christianity from Spanish Catholicism."

"Where do those differences occur, as you see it?"

"Between faith and lack of faith, and even between belief and unbelief. Menendez Pelayo has talked about the practical atheism of our Spanish Catholics. In the late sixteenth century, at the very height of the Spanish campaign on behalf of the Counter-Reformation, other Europeans used to say: 'As unbelieving as a Spaniard'."

"But in quoting that proverb, surely you oughtn't to forget that it referred to temporal actions: military and political. We are back now in what Malraux calls the domains of action and contemplation."

"Obviously I'm not talking about the kingdom of God, but on the contrary about the domain of Evil. I myself think that Evil is an abstraction. The plurality Malraux ascribes to it belongs in fact to another reality which, for me, is called the Evil One, the Devil. We know that Christ's prayer in the Gospel asks for us to be delivered from the Evil One, not from Evil: it is not the domain of Evil that is involved, but the domain of the Evil One, which means the domain of the Devil. What we call the World. Victor Hugo gave what is perhaps the best definition of the Devil when he said — I quote from memory — that he is 'the plurality of evil unified by darkness'. But if we were to say, out of a facile desire for symmetry and moral antithesis, that God is the plurality of Good unified by light, that wouldn't be true at all."

"Why not?"

"Because Good, like Evil, is an abstraction. Both notions fall into the judicial, or in other words the moral domain of Manicheism. I would venture to say that God and the Devil are beyond Good and Evil."

"Which brings us back, I feel, to Job, to the terrible anguish inflicted on our conscience by Job's situation. For me, the book of Job contains all the fundamental, existential ideas of Judaism. Job's state is an accusation directed against a God whose wrath is equalled only by his indifference. He remains silent, and only reveals himself 'gratuitously', absurdly, when Job has gone through his night of the soul."

"God wasn't there. God never enters into dialogues. With anyone. Unless it be himself. The Devil talks to everyone, except himself. In Job's dialogue with the accuser, the Devil seems to be holding a dialogue with Job, whereas in fact he is talking to his mirror. Like Narcissus. Because he believes, or pretends to believe, like Narcissus, that the image in the mirror is someone else. But that someone else isn't God!"

"You say: God wasn't there. A criminal absence!"

"Now you are slipping into those judicial and moral domains I spoke of. You are judging God. Take care, you are going further than the Devil himself. Because the Devil doesn't judge. He accuses. There is no judgment possible beyond Good and Evil. The Last Judgment is not a judgment. It is an apotheosis."

"Do you think that Job in some sense represents the human condition?"

"I think that Job possibly represents the human condition of sanctity. And shows that it too is beyond Good and Evil. That is why I once said that all the saints have held dialogues with the Devil; though I think now that their dialogues too were held with the Devil's image in the mirror. When I was talking about Malraux once, I made a pun in the hope of defining him for people who knew nothing about him. I said that in order to understand him all you need do is to join *La*

Condition humaine to *Espoir* and say: The Human Condition of Hope is Despair."

"Kierkegaard?"

"And also the Spanish philosopher Ortega y Gasset, who said: You cannot understand Christianity unless you begin from the radical form of life constituted by despair. Malraux added: and solitude. Solitude in a museum. Which means the domain of imagination. And perhaps of antimemory too. Is it possible to find our way out of history as though from some illusory labyrinth? In Malraux's *Espoir*, the despair is possibly masked by poetic illusion. An illusion called the Apocalypse, which identifies revelation with revolution. That isn't just a play on words, or rather it is precisely a transcendental play on words. Faith is a lightning flash. On Sinai as on the road to Damascus. Which is why I think that once you come down from Sinai you descend into the domain of morality, and once you have fallen from the horse too, when the lightning flash is over. Because we mustn't forget that St. Paul was a contemporary of Seneca, and that they could well have met in the streets of Rome. Through which the Devil still strolls today. When I arrived in Paris after more than fifteen years of exile in America, Malraux said to me: 'Literature doesn't exist. But neither does existentialism.'"

"Is that what you call being a phantom?"

"Victor Hugo once said that we perform the task of a man and the task of a phantom in life. Which brings us close to Nietzsche's *Wanderer and his Shadow*, and also, in consequence, to the impossibility of absolute solitude and its attendant despair. I think of Seneca when I consider, like St. Paul, the impossibility of tragedy after Christ."

"Does that mean you think, with Nietzsche, that tragedy no longer exists for man after the crucifixion? Which I don't."

"I do, yes. Tragedy, to my way of thinking, even as

André Malraux in his study, during the early 'Thirties

109

an awareness of fate, is a dramatic rhetoric quite opposed to Christianity. For Malraux, Mr. Zeus is someone we know nothing about. That doesn't mean for me that Prometheus is prophesying Christ."

"For Malraux, the face of Christ is visible only to the true believer."

"On Veronica's napkin, in other words."

"In art, Christ is either a symbol or a representation."

"In either case we are back in the realm of poetry. In the etymological sense of the word, that is: in eternal creation. Malraux is trying to escape from time and space through the dimension of imagination."

"Which is the poem . . ."

"But which is also the labyrinth of art. And that is why Malraux talks about the romance of history and his Museum without Walls, his museum of the imagination. In time as in space, Art 'desmemoriza' — takes away the memory — of history through the power of poetry. Which is why, despite the general title of his books on art, *The Psychology of Art*, Malraux is not dealing in psychology at all. He isn't a psychologist. He isn't a psychiatrist. He doesn't psychoanalyze art. He is a psychopomp. Hermetic, in the sense that the word applies to the god Hermes, and also in the sense of Hermes Trismegistes, who is the Devil."

"Beware the Sphinx's claws!"

"Then let us change the subject and talk about chimeras."

"What do you mean?"

"I mean, as Malraux says, that the enigma of art is the one we find in *Don Quixote* and *Las Meninas*. Neither Cervantes nor Velasquez is in fact giving us ambiguous or equivocal answers. Both rather pose the same question that Don Quixote puts to the Enchanted

< André Malraux, Mme du Perron, wife of the Dutch poet, Eddy du Perron, Clara Malraux (1939)

Left to right: André Malraux, Salvador de Madariaga, Denis de Rougemont, William Faulkner, W. H. Auden

José Bergamín, Paris, November 1973 >

113

Head: 'Was it truth or a dream, the account I gave of going down into the Cave of Montesinos?' The riddle at the heart of Cervantes' book can be reduced to this: the opposite of truth is not untruth but reason. To find the truth we must lose our reason. And I may also add: by searching for truth we find poetry. And the reverse of that also holds good."

"So why do you say that Don Quixote and Don Juan are not Spanish?"

"What I say is rather that they are not exclusively, typically Spanish. What does that mean: 'to be Spanish'? It reminds me of something Nietzsche said: 'To be a good German is the same thing as ceasing to be German.' And he cited Goethe as an example. I think one could likewise say that to be a good Spaniard means to cease being Spanish. And the example I would give is Cervantes. Or in our own day, Picasso."

"Is there any connection here with what Malraux calls his 'violent sense of transience'?"

"When I arrived in Paris, during my second exile from Spain, by which time I was no longer a political refugee but under offical proscription, because the Spanish government had refused me identity papers, the French police, who were very kind to me, wrote on my resident's permit: 'nationality to be decided'!"

"Your phantom again!"

"And given official recognition."

"Is it a real phantom then?"

"Unreal and irrational. In May 1968 I remember saying goodbye to Malraux outside the Palais Bourbon one day, after we'd had lunch together. As we parted, he said: 'Now I must remain here in unreality, while you go off into the irrational.' I was on my way to the Sorbonne."

"Do you believe that we were in the realm of the romance of history, as Malraux calls it, in May 1968?"

André Malraux, *Time* magazine, June 1947

"Yes, just as we were in 1936 in Spain."

"With the difference that in Spain real blood was shed."

"In Paris, the barricades were symbolic. But in Spain as in France the revolution was a revelation. In both cases a counter-revolution occurred in time to quench the fire. Only in France it happened much more quickly, almost immediately, thanks to the Communist Party."

"And afterwards?"

"Spain, which was different, became indifferent . . . and a tourist paradise."

"Saint and prostitute."

"Yes, both. You see it everywhere. Mysticism and the picaresque are traditional and inseparable in Spanish literature. But again, as with Don Quixote and Don Juan, that is something not exclusively and typically Spanish. It is typically Christian rather, in the sense in which Christianity becomes part of the romance of history. We still have the Golden Legend, the Lives of the Saints. The most saintly of all the saints, and Christ's greatest apostle, is Mary Magdalene."

"Do you believe that Christianity and its saints will still have anything to say to the coming generation?"

"More than ever before."

"And after that?"

"'Time doesn't pass: time begins,' Eluard said."

"Then taking into account that time doesn't pass but begins, if I had to draw up a spiritual genealogy for Malraux today, where would I find his roots?"

"In the *Encyclopédie* (Diderot-Rousseau), I think, and also in the line that runs from Chateaubriand

At Saint-Brieuc with Eddy du Perron, the Dutch poet and friend to whom Malraux dedicated *La Condition humaine*.

His daughter Florence >

Roland Malraux, his brother >

119

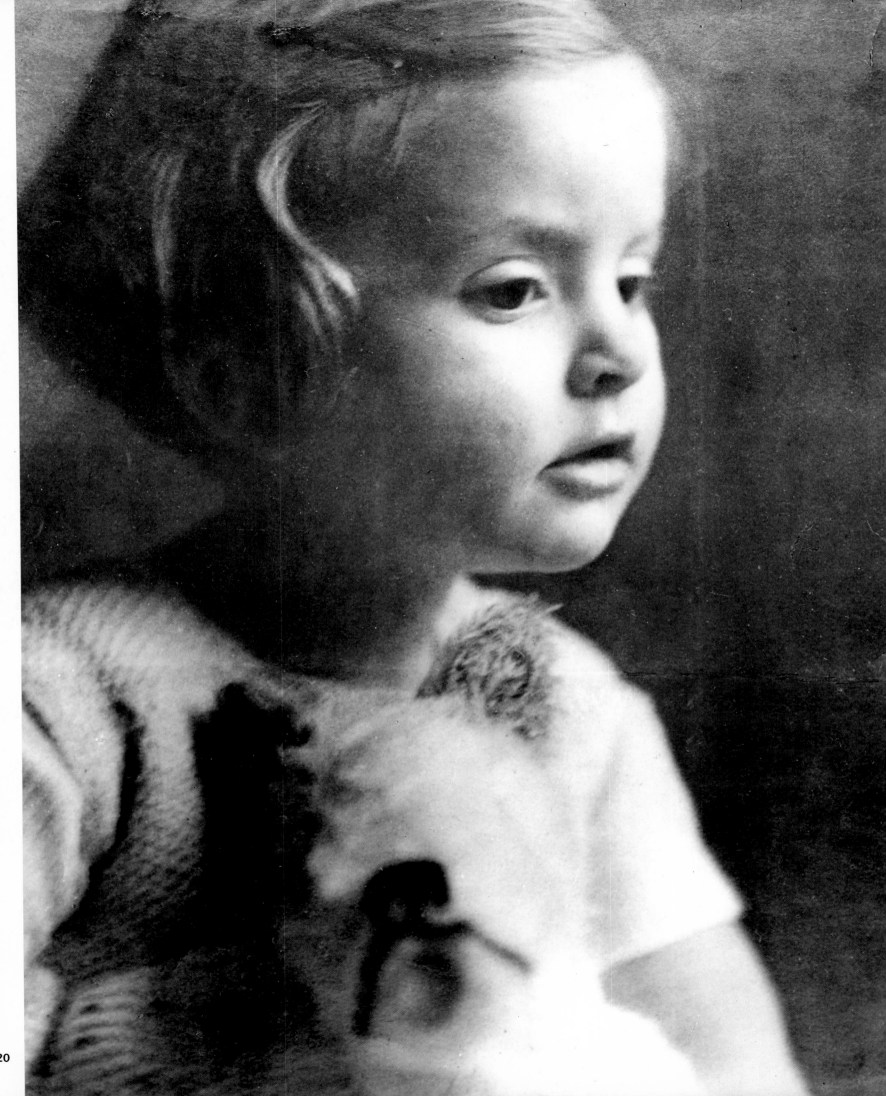

through Hugo to Barrès. Which is why Malraux tells us that he was alone, in his generation, in shocking Gide and the N.R.F. group with his defence of Hugo, who as I told Gide myself is certainly the greatest French poet to a Spaniard, and no 'alas!'."

"Do you think that the *Mémoires d'Outre-tombe*, Malraux's favourite work by Chateaubriand, falls into the realm of historical legend, of the romance of history?"

"Yes, and so does the *Génie du Christianisme*."

"And the line goes as far as Barrès?"

"Via Victor Hugo. Rémy de Gourmont called Chateaubriand the grandfather of our most savage individualists. Which means Barrès. The greatest of his grandsons."

"And Malraux?"

"I don't know what Malraux will think of my saying so, but I believe I detect the same song in his prose. The song that Barrès discovered and loved in Spain."

"What is the value of the song you hear in Malraux's *Espoir*?"

"It is the selfsame song one hears in Barrès's book *Du Sang, de la Volupté et de la Mort.* The same yet not the same. There is a great distance between Barrès and Malraux. But no break. And in that distance, as in everything that is far away from us, like Romantic poetry, there is a sense of a deeper closeness. On the surface, silence. Yet in that silence, Malraux's voice in *Espoir* brings me as it were an echo of the Barrésian tone. Malraux's *Espoir* for me is not at all the 'reporting of genius' that Camus saw in it, but a sort of black-and-white X-ray, like Picasso's *Guernica*, of the destruction that overtook Spain in 1936. Malraux's novel is at the same time an eye witness account and an accusation, both as alive today as they were thirty years ago, and even more alive. Like *Les Grands Cimetières sous la*

André Malraux with André Gide (1934), just before delivering their petition against the Nazi detention of George Dimitrov

lune by Bernanos, and even more so his *Nouvelle Histoire de Mouchette*, in which the heart of that anguished, dying Spain is still beating to this very day . . ."

"Was Malraux fond of Bernanos?"

"As fond as I was myself. Mauriac used to say that Bernanos, Maritain, Mauriac himself, and I, saved the honour of the Church during the Spanish Civil War. I'm more inclined to think that what we were trying to save then was the truth of the Spanish people, who were being sacrificed at the time with an episcopal blessing."

"You are thinking of the 1936 crusade."

"Yes. To me it was a sacrilege, and a stupidly satanic crime."

"What do you mean?"

"I mean that in Dante's Hell we see Satan chained up like a stupid monster. Because he has lost his angelic intelligence. He is his own prisoner, as someone said of the Pope. Dante also tells us that the damned in Hell 'hanno perduto il ben del'inteletto', have lost the blessing of intelligence. The Devil still hides in the Church, as the poet says; it is he who inspires its stupid politics."

"Malraux says he has never been interested in politics, only in history. How does one separate the one from the other?"

"That depends on what you mean by the term politics, and by the term history. Because, still following Malraux's line of thought, we can think of politics and history as what he terms 'domains'. Heine claimed to have been passionately interested in politics and religion almost to the exclusion of everything else. Unamuno too, because he believed them to be inseparable. But there is neither politics nor religion without history. I simply think that the politics in which Malraux has no interest is something different. It is

'Colonel Berger', Malraux in the Resistance movement, after the Alsace-Lorraine Brigade had recaptured Sainte-Odile

On the Rhine front, south of Strasbourg >

perhaps the politics of politicians. Which brings me back to Barrès and his contempt for that sort of politics. There was his book *Leurs Figures*, and I think it is to that sort of political image Malraux is referring, just like Barrès. I don't know whether those images today are the ones to which we attach the names Nixon, Brezhnev, Chou En-Lai, or Pompidou. But their faces are rather too similar for comfort to the ones Barrès depicts. Barrès, of course, wasn't as lucky as Malraux with his General. Which is why he always maintained that ironical and contemptuous dandyism of his in his political activities."

"It is through his poetic vision, like Dante in his day, that Malraux conceives and interprets our world."

"But through what stained glass window does it come to us? Mallarmé said that stained glass windows are either art or mysticity."

"As far as the art is concerned I follow you. But mysticity? What mysticity?"

"That of the mystery. Which is my cue for silence, since the mystery does not speak. And that is why the mystery in the works of the mystics keeps its silence. Meaning that it becomes a guardian of silence as of a treasure. A treasure that it must guard out of generosity and not out of avarice. But if the true mystic must remain silent to avoid self-betrayal, the poet on the contrary speaks continually, and must continually speak. And of the mystery, but mysteriously. When Mallarmé says that the window must be art or mysticity, he doesn't mean that mysticity betrays the windowmaker's art. That art, interposed between the light and our eyes — and this is what Malraux grasped so lucidly — makes it possible for us to receive a vision of the mysterious light without betraying that light and without blinding us. Symbolically, in our cathedrals, the mysticity of the glass becomes as it were a technique for rendering the luminous transparency of the sun possible for mortal eyes. And the sun, in this poetic symbolics, is God. It was Malraux who made me aware of the beauty of the Romanesque crucifixion window in the Gothic cathedral of Poitiers, which is no less fine than that of the Holy

André Malraux at the NRF with Marcel Arland, Jules Supervielle, Jean Paulhan and Paul Valéry

Virgin in Chartres. So that when Mallarmé says 'art or mysticity', for me that means that there can be no art without mysticity. Luminous or shadowy. The play of light and darkness in our mystic cathedrals is at the same time an invitation to prayer and that divine vision in which the Devil too can snare us. Our cathedrals, like St. Teresa's and St. John of the Cross's *Mistica Teologia*, by attempting to penetrate the Divine Mystery can also become transformed into a Satanic trap."

"Why do you always insist on the presence of the Devil within the Church?"

"Because that is his favorite haunt. That is where he can both hide and show himself to best effect. Our present Pope, Paul VI, an admirable writer, expressed it very well on the occasion of his ninth anniversary in office. With poetic accuracy, saying that it was the Devil, 'that mysterious being', who had spoiled the fruits of the Council. He denounced the presence of the Devil at the end of the council, and with striking literary precision, just as his predecessor, St. John XXIII, issued his warning at its outset that when they closed the doors, the Devil might have been shut in with them. At the end of the Council, Paul VI said, at the time when we were expecting to see a new day of peace and sunlight dawning, we find ourselves still in darkness. Wrapped in storm clouds. What happened? And he added: 'I tell you this in confidence, what happened is that that mysterious being (the Devil) appeared to spoil and wither the fruits of the Council.' It is a story that Bernanos would have appreciated enormously. Malraux too, I think. And since I have returned to Bernanos I will return to Dante too. With reference to hope and despair. We were saying a moment ago that there is no hope without despair, and I made a sort of pun to express the idea that the human condition of hope, according to Malraux, is despair. And that is true, just as its inverse is also. There can be no despair without hope. Monsieur de La Palice would certainly have assented to that. However, if I am repeating myself it is because I still remember the inscription Bernanos wrote for me in a copy of his *Grands Cimetières sous la Lune* on the very

André Malraux (1945)

131

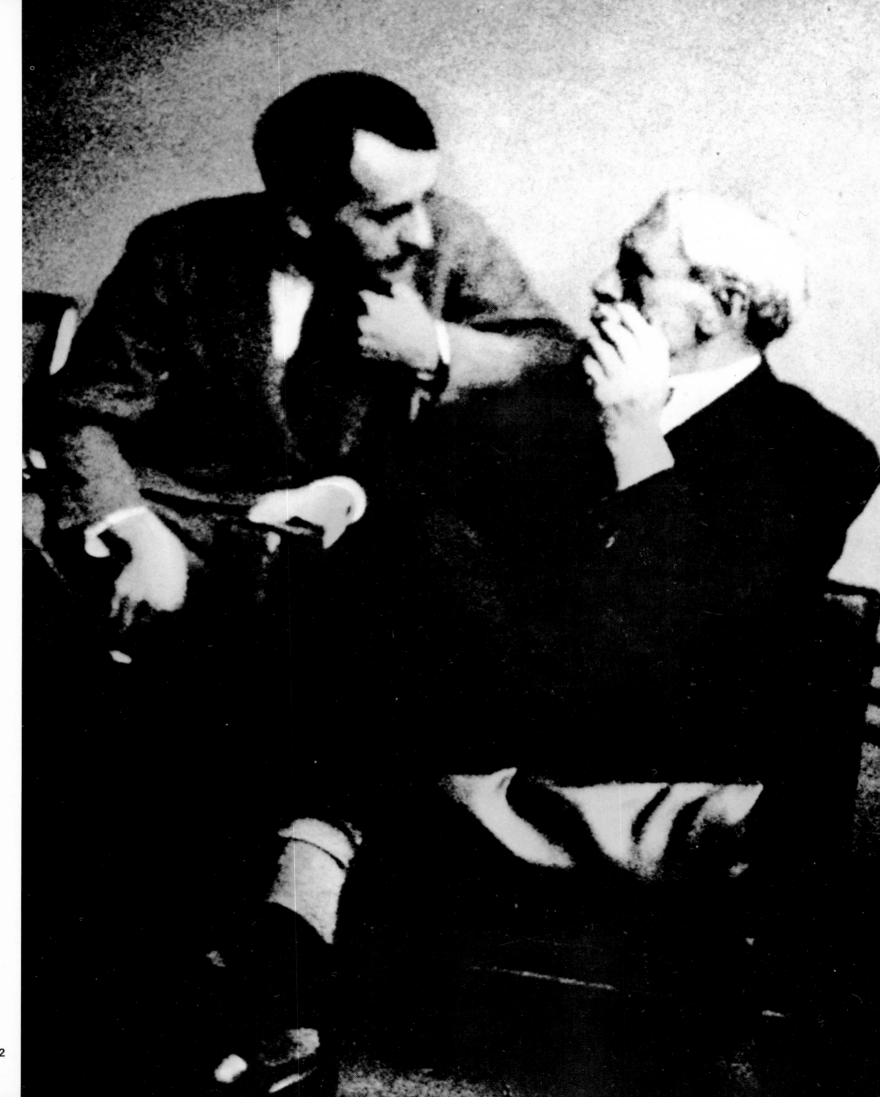

eve of his departure in 1937. It said: 'In heartfelt expectation and longing for peace'. The war in Spain had just begun. The World War was still to come. Well! Expectation and longing are not hope. Is hope a domain too, as Malraux would say? An abstraction? A sovereign abstraction? In Dante's sacred poem, we read on the shadowy scroll over the Gates of Hell: *Lasciate ognie esperanze voi che entrate*, and I take it that it is expectation, the French *espérance*, they must abandon, not *l'espoir*, hope in its absolute form. Though we ought to note that the same words could also perfectly well be placed, in letters of light, above the Gates of Heaven. Waiting, expectation, belong to Purgatory alone. Does hope reside nowhere then? In which case what can despair mean?"

"The story about the Devil you told just now, the one you said Bernanos and Malraux would have appreciated, doesn't it fall into the domain of history?"

"One can fall into history as into a well. It is sometimes at the bottom of a well that we must go to search for truth. Like Don Quixote down in the Cave of Montesinos. But the Pope didn't say whether what he said in confidence is true or not. Though he does say: 'That is how it happened.' Of course he was not claiming infallibility in this case. His sincerity is not in doubt, however. And in any case, his testimony is the most valid we have. I myself would venture to say that the Catholic Church's Council has lost its divine face. Much more so than during the Council of Trent, in my opinion. Because it has made itself temporal, worldly, social, before everything and on every subject. Every time the Devil hears the word *aggiornamento* I hear his laughter, as loud and mocking as that of Homer's gods. Merleau-Ponty once cited me in his book *Sens et Non-Sens* as an example of a Catholic who has tried to escape his external ambiguity without perhaps realizing that he is falling into an internal ambiguity. Which was an accurate enough observation. And I wonder myself whether the Catholic Church, in attempting without repentance to rectify its equivocal conduct in the temporal sphere, in the world, in order to remove that equivocation at source, whether it does not fall into a

André Malraux and Paul Valéry (1939)

José Bergamín, Paris, November 1973 >

133

more serious equivocation still, one that I will term internal, invisible, one in which it may betray its supernatural truth and even the Kingdom of God, since it is betraying itself. Merleau-Ponty left us a posthumous book on the invisible and the visible. The great mystic and Christian poet Raymond Lulle wrote: 'There is no visible man.' What is visible in man is his phantom. What is visible in the invisible, supernatural, divine, non-temporal Church is likewise its phantom. 'My Church', Bernanos used to say, 'is the Church of the Saints.' There is no other true Christian and Catholic Church. It is the phantom of the Catholic Church that pursues and is pursued, like all phantoms. But when the sun appears at cockcrow, the proverb says (and the sun is God), the phantom flies. And as another proverb significantly has it: 'All savage beasts do fly'."

"This invisible Church, this invisible man you are talking about, they are illusions for the person who isn't a believer."

"The man who doesn't believe doesn't exist. He may be living but he is non-existent. In order to win votes in their electoral campaigns, the French Communists used to say: 'Believers and non-believers'. They didn't dare say unbelievers. In their fear of mystery — and many other things that aren't mysterious at all — they didn't even dare to conceive of unbelief as a reality. Just as, despite their Marxism, they daren't think the fact that atheism can't exist without God. Among the Spanish lower classes, when they want to poke fun at the idea of an atheism without God, they say: 'I'm an atheist, thank God!'"

"So illusion, for you, is not the opposite of reality?"

"Absolutely not. It is rather the only method of penetrating reality. In the same way that untruth, as I said earlier, is not the opposite of truth but its transparent mask (as Nietzsche and Wilde both thought), so illusion is not the opposite of reality but again its transparent mask. Which is why the ages of illusion are childhood and old age. And those are precisely the times when we are nearer to reality, because we are

André Malraux, Minister of Information, and Vladimir Clémentis, Czech Foreign Minister, at the signing of the Franco-Czech treaty (1945)

137

nearer, it seems, to the frontiers of that nothingness from which we come and into which we go. But this word 'néant' doesn't mean anything because it means *nothing*, 'nada'. But that nothing, that *nada*, is everything. And that everything is God. We are as close to God in childhood as we are in old age. As we leave childhood so we move further from Him. I once wrote a little poem in which I said that we don't return to childhood when we grow old, but that our childhood has in fact kept pace very slowly beside us, all through our youth, waiting to rejoin us when the bustle of our prime is past. That is what poets and mystics have continually told us: that this illusion of life is the reality. And especially the Christian poets, Dante, Shakespeare, Cervantes, Calderón, St. Teresa, St. John of the Cross . . ."

"After Job, Isaiah, David . . ."

"There would have been no Christian poets without them. But then there would have been no Christ without them either. And now I must ask Malraux's forgiveness for what I am about to say. What disturbs me always in him, and sometimes distresses me greatly, is his youthfulness. As though he had forgotten ever being a child, and because he is so young, somehow refuses, perhaps, to be old.

> La maladie et la mort font des cendres
> De tout ce feu qui pour nous flamboya. [1]

[1]Sickness and death make ashes
Of all that fire that flamed for us.

"Baudelaire, who died young, tells us in those two magnificent lines what youth really means. In 1968, Malraux tells us, those who exploded into protest throughout the world were all young. Which is true. And yet I find myself thinking of the old people and the children in the Prague spring rising, so close, for me, to the old people and children of Madrid in the summer of 1936. Today, when I wander through some sleepy little Spanish village, deserted by its youth, where there are none but old people and children to be seen, I think I catch in their eyes a tiny, living flame, underlined sometimes by a mocking smile. But no ashes."

We parted at the hour when the *sereno* makes his last round through the dream of old Madrid. Yet José Bergamín insisted, as a last gift from the *victima* to his *verdugo*, his tormentor, on guiding me through those deserted alleys, past the houses of Cervantes, Calderón, and Quevedo, which between three and five in the morning, with only a hundred yards between them, resume their quiet dialogues that cease only with the first gleams of dawn. Dialogues in which José Bergamín quite naturally takes his part.

André Malraux and
Madeleine, his third wife
(1947)

André Malraux (1956) >

Lightning in the night

Un relámpago de luz
Que el aire de sombra escribe.
Calderón

Florence in August splendour has transformed the voluptuous Arno into a trickle of water that runs through the city in quavers, minims, crotchets and semi-quavers. It no longer thunders. It sings. It sings of Florence, the sovereign city.

Impossible to weary of gazing down on it from one of its encircling hills, jealous guardians of the treasures it contains. Florence basks and relaxes, serene and carefree in the westering light.

I was determined to see Florence again before my next interview with André Malraux.

Bergamín had said: "Tragedy, even as consciousness of fate, is a dramatic rhetoric quite opposed to Christianity." Contemplating the work of the divine Angelico, one can only accept that statement. His Virgins with child convey a hidden anguish, a heart-rending tension. They have the same foreknowledge that gives his nativities their burden of inevitability. And then, by some strange metamorphosis, the anguish and the expectation are transformed into liberated tenderness as that same Virgin contemplates, no longer her Son lying at her feet, but doubtless something she alone can see, a new order of things. Does that emotion in which she is now gripped still belong to our human order?

Is what she alone of those present can perceive still part of what we call happiness? Or is it already beatitude? "Blessed be the sad hour of the fulfilment", Miloscz wrote. The human is reconciled here with the divine.

Surrounded once more by so many works of Italian art, from the Quattrocento to the Settecento, I couldn't help comparing them with the legacy of Spain. Malraux's vision in *Le Triangle noir* suddenly found its justification here: "Confronted with Italy, the language of Spain at its greatest has always been the same; in that Rome where El Greco expressed regret over Michelangelo's inadequacy as a painter, where Velasquez, forced into giving an opinion of Raphael, had simply said: 'I just don't like that sort of thing!', one can imagine Goya, faced with a *Trial of Christ* by Magnasco, thinking: 'How good that would be, if it were true . . .'"

André Malraux, Minister of
State for Cultural Affairs
(1967)

We met again at the same time and in the same immutable setting as before.

This time, no March showers in June but the splendour of summer in decline. The ritual of our second interview was identical with that two months before. Wires, lamps, tapes, and the bizarre parasol were now all familiar. André Malraux helped with the setting up.

We talked about Madrid, about Venice and its Tintorettos, then about Florence, from which I had sent him my outline notes for this second meeting.

"I suggested recently that you might look into the notion of happiness, which you dismiss in your work with some contempt. You answered that you would rather talk about serenity."

"Serenity is a clear notion, whereas happiness, for me, is an unintelligible one. The word happiness is rather like the word freedom: it has a meaning in a context. Freedom, on its own, is an idiotic word, whereas freedoms, in the plural, isn't at all. Freedom of expression, now, that's not an idiotic expression, nor is the freedom of the citizen. But freedom in itself — I've already said this somewhere — is one of what I call the trap words. They have an enormous importance in every civilization (though they're not always the same ones, of course!); their appeal is so powerful that they suck everything else into them. That's the secret of their strength, and it's not just a chance process either. In every civilization the number one trap word is *God*, because whatever the civilization, whatever the religion, that one word always really expresses a good four or five different notions. For example, in Christianity it means: *justice* (in the sense of the Last Judgment) and *creation*, which are distinct notions. *Absolute*, another distinct notion. *Love*, a totally separate notion. And others as well. Within every religion, of course, the great minds have always defined what they were talking about; St. Thomas doesn't say love when he means creation. But in everyday language the opposite is true: everything always implies everything else. In our own day, I would suggest you take a look at the words progress — revolution — democracy. I hope that a hundred years from now someone will analyze the keywords of our civilization, of the civilization, let's say, that was born with the machine. The word happiness would be on that list. But not serenity, because in every civilization the meaning of the word serenity can be precisely circumscribed. Let's say that some civilizations have gone for arts of serenity, and others for arts of drama. Is Chinese art the same as Romanesque art? Obviously not. We don't have any analysis of serenity, and I think it is badly needed. It would help us to understand Far Eastern painting much better. We must be careful to remember that we know their sculpture far better. There have been photographs of the great Buddhist caves, but colour reproduction of the paintings is only recent — and approximate. In fact there's not a single reasonably adequate work on Far Eastern painting available to students, even now, outside the major libraries. Yet there are only two important bodies of painting in the world: ours and theirs. What is there apart from that? Either charming Indian and Persian miniatures, or else the great Indian and Chinese religious frescoes. They certainly count, of course, but they aren't exactly what a painter would call painting. If you asked Chagall: what do you think of the Ajanta frescoes?, he would answer: I think they were done by a magnificent artist, but what a pity he wasn't a painter! (Which is what he says in fact about Picasso.) And what's more he wouldn't be wrong, because 'painting' is another trap word. When Chagall talks about the chemistry of colour he means the relationships between his colours. Everyone accepts that stridency, dissonance, harmony, are fundamental notions in his work. Yet the notions of stridency and dissonance are unknown in the Far East. All that is just us. Like the orchestra. So that when it comes to analyzing Chinese and Japanese painting we haven't much in the way of tools. Even if you happen to know their painting from having seen it out there, it's still at a great remove from us, because we have this tendency to look at any painting as though it's a modern picture. And in this case that's difficult. We can sense clearly enough the link between their painting and ideographic writing. But take the Eccentrics — they were painters of the seventeenth and eighteenth centuries. Can we look at them as we look at . . . whom? Picasso. It just isn't possible. Lautrec? . . . But we know it's something completely different. Recently, at the Fondation Maeght, you saw one of the greatest examples of the Far Eastern tradition: the *Shigemori*. When you stand in front of it, you realize at once that it has nothing in common with a Flemish primitive; I say a Flemish primitive because the character in black, with the dark head and background, suggests that analogy. But it is something utterly different. So what was it all based on? On a truth, on a self-evident fact accepted without argument by the entire Far East; and it existed before Buddhism. That fundamental and self-evident fact was the existence of an *Inner Reality*. With capital letters. I repeat: it was not something you could argue about. So what was the purpose of painting? For painters, it was a snare they set for that Inner Reality, their way of catching it. In other words, of grasping the essential in everything. Everything except what had been made by the hand of man. You can paint rocks, you can invent rocks (even though, in Western terms, one wouldn't say that they are alive), you can paint still-lifes with fruit, perhaps

with vegetables; but you can't paint a still-life with a violin, or its case; that would be the end of everything! Anything artificially created, made by man, has no place in painting. Man-made things have no Inner Reality. In the sense in which we Westerners would say they have no soul. For Takanobu, the painter of *Shigemori*, it was not a matter of knowing what the individual Inner Reality of Prince Shigemori was, but of knowing how to insert a sign that is the prince's effigy into the supreme Reality. The prince becomes other than himself because the correlation of the colours, lines, etc. of life is abolished in favour of another correlation, that of painting; but this new correlation permits the spectator to enter into communion with the Inner Reality of the universe. Which sounds complicated, but isn't really, if we think of Greece.

"In Greece, as in China or Japan, there was a cosmos. And cosmos means order, an ordered universe, it's the same thing. And Greek artists made choices, like the Chinese painters: they eliminated what they decided to eliminate. The sculptor was attracted by a certain woman. What was he going to use that feeling for? Certainly not to make a portrait of her. There are no Greek portraits from the great classical era. He was going to do an Aphrodite, no question of anything else. And when he had sculpted his Aphrodite, then he had fixed the divine essence of the lady in question. Or, if you like, he had made use of the lady to fix a reflection of the divine essence. Which was that of the cosmos, of absolute order. Hence the idea of the beautiful. It is a procedure that makes it easier for us to understand the Far Eastern procedure too. I remember telling you once a rather fascinating story, that of the so-called 'true' trial of Phryne. You know the original legend: Phryne posed for an Aphrodite, and she was therefore guilty of a crime, because no woman ought to pose for a goddess. She was in danger of the death sentence. So she comes before the Areopagus, she removes her veils, and she is so beautiful that the court acquits her. The other version, the 'legend of the truth', is much more interesting: again she removes her veils, but then she says: you can see only too well that I am *not* the goddess! Because she is like the statue, but the statue is not a likeness of her. No statue is ever a likeness of a mortal. And they acquit her. That second legend is crucial. You cannot begin to apprehend the spirit of Greek sculpture, up to and including Phidias, if you assume that the statue could possibly have been Phryne. Just remember that there is not a single portrait-statue of a woman from the classical era, not one. All goddesses."

I couldn't help thinking, however interesting the arguments he had just expounded, that Malraux was to some extent simply dismissing my first question. Or was that simply a result of my own feverish impatience to hear

him speak other words, words that would elucidate in a single flash the questions that constantly gnaw in all our deepest hearts?

But he had taught me that "man begins with the other", and I was discovering once again that his analyses of art are also self-analyses, analyses of man himself, conducted always with "an honest determination to find out the facts".

"Greek sculpture communicates the serenity you spoke of earlier."

"Any cosmos implies a serenity."

"Something you find very rarely, nevertheless, in Christian art."

"The Christian universe is a dramatic universe. Even that of the Old Testament. As for that of the New, just think what the significance must be for Buddhist eyes that its symbol is the cross — an instrument of torture. Though of course it is not exclusively a dramatic universe, it is not all conflict. You were right to mention Fra Angelico just now. There is a part of the Christian soul that sometimes rediscovers the cosmos. You'll find all the theory of it in Nicholas of Cusa, a great philosopher. His book is called *De Docta Ignorantia*. It was after him that the 'reconciled man' expressed in Raphael was generally proclaimed. Angelico's man was also reconciled. There are periods when Christianity loses its devil. The first time being probably in Franciscan art. The immense poetic power of 'my sister the rain' is a cosmos in its own way. But what about Gothic art, you may say. The reconciled Christ in Chartres — the one in the South transept, not the one in the Portail Royal — is contemporary with St. Francis's death, and therefore with a time when the saint's teachings were completely familiar. Even Giotto's universe, which was Franciscan in spirit, is a reconciled world, especially if you compare it with that of the painting that precedes it, in other words with Cimabue, or even Duccio. Moreover it was to account for him that 'Nature' was invented: a term that held no suggestion of going out and painting in the field but expressed the break with Byzantium."

"Isn't art in general — and that of the Italian Renaissance in particular — in all its various and multiple forms, in various degrees of intensity, always a perpetually renewed attempt to effect a reconciliation between man and cosmos? The attempts for the most part fail, but their failures are a reflection at the highest level of the failure of love. (The story of the Jews and more precisely that of Christ are our highest testimony to that.) So could we not say that art's failures also tend to prove that reconciliation is a perpetual metamorphosis?"

"That depends on the moment in time. And it applies only to Italy. Certainly not to Goya."

"Not to Goya. But to the Italian Seicento."

"Let's begin with Tuscan art, and keep things simple. First, there are all the pre-Franciscan things: a Byzantine art. Then the break. Cimabue and Giotto. In other words Assisi. On the universe of Giotto I'm in agreement with you. If it isn't a reconciled world as yet, then it is at any rate an awe-inspiring glimpse of reconciliation to come. There have been occasions when art, the resources specific to art, have resolved what the resources of thought have been unable to resolve. After all, one may say that there is something in Giotto much more reconciled than in contemporary writing. Because the great mind contemporary with Giotto was Dante . . . Giotto's influence fills the century. Then we come to Masaccio, and all those painters to whom he was a guiding light. And here the cap doesn't fit so well. Castagno is inclined to be tragic; Uccello, we have to be careful. Piero della Francesca, it depends on which works you pick; however, there is that superb 'severe style', as we say of the transitional pre-Phidias style in Greece, there is the Queen of Sheba's great white cloak. Especially when you see what it developed from. Someone has at last succeeded in photographing the frescoes of his predecessor in illustrating the Discovery of the Cross, the theme of Piero's fresco in Arezzo. The perspective is different, the whole viewpoint is different, the spirit is medieval. Piero possesses at least the serenity of majesty. But have you seen the Borgo fresco? The reproductions give you no idea, and it can't be moved. There you can see that he has quite clearly emulated the art of the icons. There's no doubt whatever. The face of the risen Christ is painted twice as wide as any real face in order to achieve the hypnotic effect of those Pantocrator eyes, the eyes you see in the great Sicilian mosaics. With Angelico there can be no doubt . . . What he gives us isn't man reconciled with the pagan world, but it is man forgiven. In some paintings at least, particularly the one in the Louvre. And notice that it depicts the coronation of the Virgin, an attempt at a cosmos, with encircling angels . . ."

"In every attempt at artistic creation, whether it's a matter of the Far Eastern universe and sensibility or of Western aspiration clothed in totally different forms, isn't there an identical quest for transcendence and the absolute? A quest that creates a certain oneness, far beyond periods and styles, in the question that man is hurling at the cosmos?"

"I don't want to rush my answer here, because you seem to me to be asking two rather different questions.

Doctor *honoris causa* of Oxford University (1967)

148

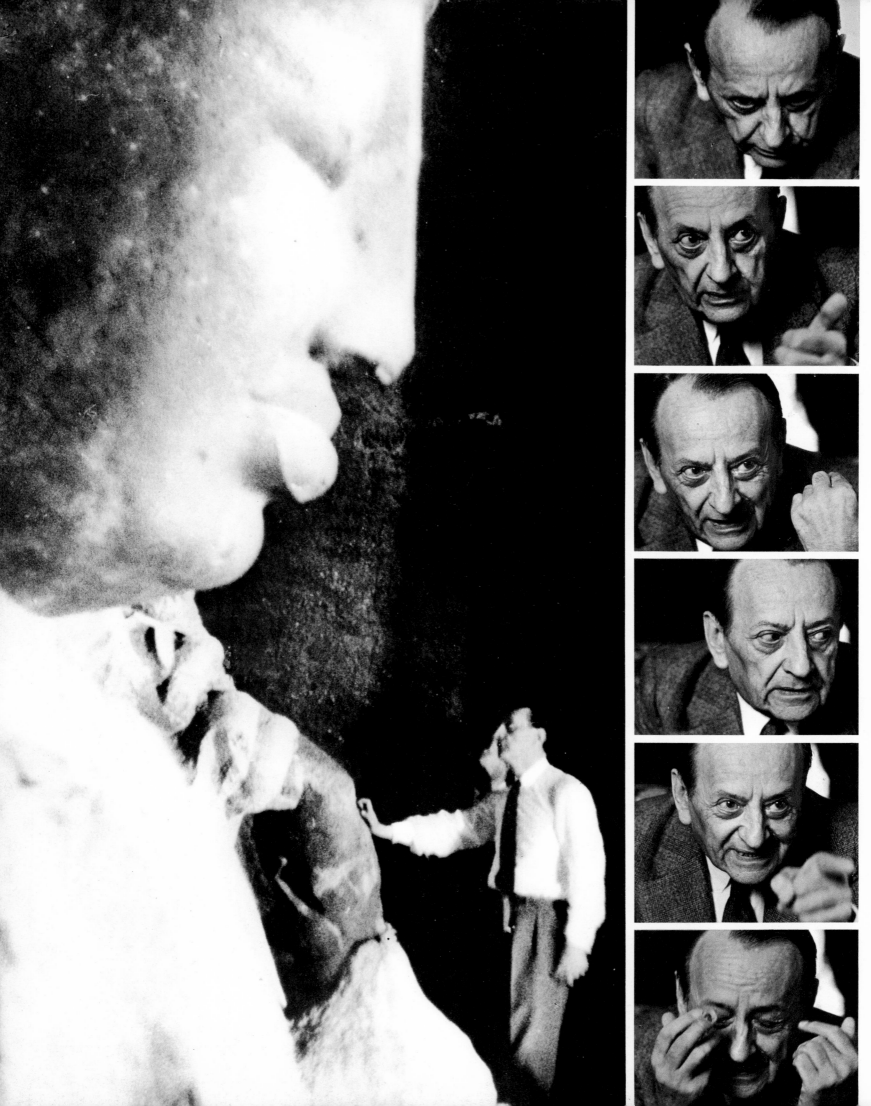

The first is concerned with artistic creation as such, the second is about the Museum without Walls. I mean that artistic creations, whether we like it or not, are there in front of us, not as a result of any decision we have taken but just because that's how it is. I mean: you didn't in any way choose to admire Fra Angelico. That's how it was."

"The work is a summons, as Claudel used to say."

"And Claudel was right. Works of art are presences, they are always now. Angelico is a presence. And the totality of those presences within you, established or latent, does constitute a question. A question dependent upon the totality of art as we receive it, which is to say through a metamorphosis, one that is at the same time historical like that of eras in history and also channeled by our own art. Does that give you a basic fact corresponding to the area you were asking about? (Because putting it into a precise form is difficult; but I see what you are getting at.) The answer is certainly yes: all art combines in us to form a question. Now your second question, a very different one: is all artistic creation directed towards the same goal? I don't think so. I think that art has been directed towards a number of fairly diverse goals, and that our own Museum without Walls is arranged in accordance with a cosmos that is specifically our own. *The Wounded Lioness*, one of the masterpieces of the most savage civilizations the world has ever known, is for us a figure of pity. The totality of art subjects the individual work to a metamorphosis, then slips it back into its place as though it had never touched it. The case of Goya is extraordinary. *The Third of May, 1808* is one of the most dramatic paintings in existence. Yet when we look at it we are not looking at an appalling massacre."

"Yes. There is an alienation effect operating between the work and the person looking at it."

"There is drama there, in the sense that there is drama in a crucifix, that yes, but there is no agonizing spectacle, what we see is not of that nature at all. There remains creation itself. That's something I'm working on at the moment. It was one of my conversations with Picasso: I believe in a certain continuous will to creation throughout man's history. It transcends the various civilizations. But does it possess an internal power forcing it to maintain itself through future civilizations, or is it the process of metamorphosis that causes us to describe as creations the principal works it selects? The maternal instinct goes on from civilization to civilization likewise; but that is biological. What we know of Egypt in the second millennium BC bears little resemblance to our own world, but the mother love

< In India, in 1958

< André Malraux at Elephanta, India, in 1958.

With Jawaharlal Nehru

they experienced was doubtless very like our own. And there is another permanent thread running through the centuries: man's ability to question his universe . . ."

"And does the reply to that questioning transcend civilizations?"

"The results of our questioning don't transcend civilizations. Unless it be by metamorphosis. But questioning the universe, that isn't something we invented. Man took a hundred thousand years to invent the snare, and possibly the grave, but he nevertheless invented them. At the present time something rather odd is happening. Our experts have begun to flirt with the idea that the emergence of true man could have taken place somewhere around the thirtieth millennium BC. With the first of the hominidae occurring in the six hundredth millennium or so. And these new datings aren't fanciful either, because Carbon-14, though it's only moderately useful for dating, say, some Roman thing (datings only accurate to within 500 years), becomes a serious tool when you're counting in millennia. And if this working hypothesis turns out to be well-founded, then that makes man contemporaneous with art."

"Contemporaneous with art?"

"Yes, with art. The thirtieth millennium BC, that's the cave fertility goddesses. Which is fairly amazing, you must admit. Because the experts who've put forward those dates aren't interested in art. Their work was undertaken purely in order to answer their own questions, anthropological ones. They are trying to fix the exact point at which man emerged from the hominidae. And it looks as if they've narrowed it down to the thirtieth millennium. While at the same time the dates of Lascaux, Altamira, and similar caves, are being put later and later . . . Lascaux, as you know, was originally put in the fortieth millennium, now it's down to the twenty-first."

"A considerable difference, clearly. Do you think that in the history of art on the one hand, and in the self-searching of our art today on the other, we may perhaps find a source of rebirth, perhaps heralding new values capable of establishing the constants of a new civilization?"

"I think that what art carries within it, the thing you are interested in, isn't historical. We have needed history . . ."

"Then what art carries within it is in the last resort non-temporal?"

"We shall come to that . . . We have needed history because it is very tempting to make the human adventure intelligible. And besides, almost all great artists start from somewhere and go somewhere. Take Assisi: when you see how Giotto emerges from Cimabue, then you're really learning something. When Picasso tells you: there were only two painters who interested me, Cézanne and Van Gogh, that really means something. From that point of view the history of art is irreplaceable. But from there to claiming art to be a product of history is a long step. The nineteenth century did a great deal of work in that line. Even before Marx: Hegel and Taine . . . And after them we had Marx and co. But in fact, the images a period produces, and whatever it is that makes certain of those images works of art, are not of the same nature. Of course, art is problematic for us, but only insofar as it is creation, not in the area of so-called artistic production. And historical conditioning applies solely to the latter. And I must say that I prefer to see serious Hegelians or Marxists working on their 'quantity becoming quality' rather than having to read those labels you used to find in the Moscow galleries in 1934, such as 'Cézanne (Paul); period of falling interest rate'."

"Which is not without its humor today . . ."

"The work of Taddeo Gaddi, a minor follower of Giotto, was conditioned by exactly the same historical circumstances as that of Giotto himself. But the fact that Giotto conceived the idea of a continuous outline to define all his figures, his trees, etc., in accordance with what he called nature, instead of working on a gold background and carrying on the Byzantine style . . . that creation, that discovery was not inscribed on the tail of any comet. No Marxism, no theory of historical conditioning can account for creation. You see that clearly in literature. There's nothing to stop you making sociology out of Romanticism, and not idiotic sociology either, Marxist or otherwise, but the historical conditioning of the sources of metaphor in Victor Hugo won't account for its existence. In the case of the painter, the irreducible fact comparable to the metaphor would be the relationship of his colours, the style of drawing — any specific element of style. I'll tell you about something that you can see now in Pisa or Avignon: shelling during the war has destroyed a number of the frescoes there and left only what the Italians call the *sinopie*. We translate that as sketches, but it's not absolutely accurate. You'll see why. When Giotto was going to do a fresco, he began by painting it in sanguine. That's the *sinopia*. Then over that he spread the plaster on to which he was going to paint the fresco itself. And because the wartime shellings have in many cases shattered the frescoes without destroying the *sinopie*, they are now

exposed. You can see yards and yards of it, especially at the Campo Santo in Pisa. And you immediately notice something fascinating: that the Trecento Tuscans didn't use a continuous line in those sketches. The continuous line was used for the frescoes, but the one used for the sketches is a broken line, not so very different from our own. So the continuous line was a stylistic invention, of the same nature as the Byzantine hieraticism. Just as the Byzantines consciously chose the hieratic style of their icons, so Florence consciously chose its distinctive style, which sixteenth-century historians elected to call primitive. Those who wrote about Giotto in the late fourteenth century don't talk about him as a primitive at all; it was Vasari who first had the idea of turning him into a primitive genius. A Romanesque drawing has also been discovered (there is only the one), and its line too is relatively broken. We have very few drawings from the periods when you could only draw on precious materials. The Egyptians, however, did drawings on pebbles and pottery tiles, the *ostraca*, which we know. And there is no question of their being in the famous Egyptian style, totally calculated and executed with a continuous line. For themselves, Egyptian draughtsmen didn't draw like that at all. That sort of drawing belonged to a style, in no way to a vision."

Silence. I noticed suddenly that the little Braque was no longer in its place. Had it been put somewhere else in the room? No. It had simply gone to the hills above Saint Paul de Vence to take part, for the space of a summer, in the Museum without Walls that the Fondation Maeght had set up there in honour of its creator.

"Does modern art after Picasso, after Braque, continue to move you? And do you still follow the efforts of the artists of today? Do you see any new movements forming among the newcomers, in France or elsewhere?"

"Clearly no movement has appeared since Cubism with that kind of importance. The problem posed by anti-art is serious, but of a different kind. I do feel it's a pity that the works in the Biennale des Jeunes are no longer chosen by national juries. What is happening in painting, taking the world as a whole? You don't really know. And neither do I. We are obliged to be wary of the art magazines, because they are inevitably biased. The most interesting painting from several Moslem countries is a slightly naïve kind of expressionism. Now the Moroccan naïfs are very interesting. But the photographs you see in the art magazines look like . . . Well, let's say Picasso. The critical trends in the Biennale des Jeunes are all predetermined these days; the artists do what they can, it's not them I'm complaining about, because at least they've invented a new category — the non-category; it was the cleverest thing they could do. They know that however hard they try to keep up with any particular trend they'll never really succeed, so they let the trends get on without them, and the 'non-competitor' is now an accepted category. So they're doing the best they can, but it does mean that the Biennale's old function as a sort of horticultural 'trial' has been lost. You asked just now if there are any particular newcomers I like. My answer is that I can't see any newcomers. A few in music . . . In architecture I can see nothing of any importance that isn't already generally accepted. Of course Niemeyer has talent, but he must be over sixty-five now. He studied with Le Corbusier.''

"You were one of the first to discover Brasilia, weren't you?"

"Yes. I inaugurated it. Though don't forget that the general plan was done by Costa. It's very good. But apparently the whole thing is still not working. Which could make a tremendous film, because if Brasilia is ever abandoned there would be nothing left but its little cowboy district, and in five years the jungle would have completely swamped the rest . . .''

He glanced out over the park, where the outlines of the trees were becoming stronger in the already fading light, adding weight to the volumes. Moderation and harmony.

André Malraux seemed to me astonishingly young. I heard Bergamín's voice again: "Now I must ask Malraux's forgiveness for what I am about to say. What disturbs me always in him, and sometimes distresses me greatly, is his youthfulness. As though he had forgotten ever being a child, and because he is so young, some-how refuses, perhaps, to be old." Malraux said:

"That's him speaking, isn't it?"

"Yes."

"I'm not at all sure I understand very clearly what he means. Young as opposed to what? 'Young' is a word that carries its own power index, as it were, it has a golden haze about it, but it doesn't really have any meaning unless we also say 'old'. Nowadays the notion of old age has been somewhat obscured. It was rela- tively clear a hundred and fifty years ago, for a variety of reasons. In the first place, by the age of about fifty, and even if you weren't particularly religious, you began thinking about the salvation of your soul. The trade in tracts preparing people for death was as flourishing then as the so-called popular literature on sex education is today. You went into training for death. And also,

André Malraux, Cabinet Minister (1959)

157

158

< André Malraux, in 1965

With Le Corbusier

because of the prevalence of disease, and especially tooth decay, people of fifty were physically affected. They were no longer the same. Whereas many men of seventy these days look very much as they did when they were fifty. In the old days, the majority of Frenchmen no longer lived the same sort of life once they reached fifty; they were physically no longer the same. Those two differences aside, there is still, I suppose, the general weakening of the powers that comes with old age. Sometimes it does, sometimes it doesn't. Sometimes both in the same person."

"The salvation you mentioned, does that imply the notion of sacrifice?"

"I am more inclined to consider your question from another angle and ask: what does 'salvation' mean outside the Christian context? It certainly means something — something it would be interesting to examine and clarify. Where the Far East is concerned it would be communion with the world essence. Which implies a separation from the world in the Christian sense, a separation that would give us one point in common with the Christian way of life: the retreat. You don't enter into communion with the world essence as a Samurai."

"The life of action you have led, all the constant activities entailed in your attempt to elucidate the civilizations that have preceded ours, seem to have led you to that state of communion."

"True communion, I believe, is nevertheless that found in the great religions, even in a religion without a god. In the Far East it was a religion without a god, that of the Chinese cosmos and world essence, that powered Buddhist art; it wasn't Buddhism that brought the world essence. There are many Taoist texts anterior to Chinese Buddhism. When Dhyāna arrived in China to become Ch'an, before becoming the Japanese Zen, the transformation of Buddhism by the fundamental non-Buddhist elements is very clear indeed . . . But your idea was: what does Salvation mean?"

"From *La Condition humaine* to *Les Chênes qu'on abat*, including your *Antimémoires* and books on art, your whole work seems to me to have been a quest for salvation."

"What I've written about art, so be it. It was relatively precise because I had as my point of departure the fact that we had revived the religious arts, since the deeper we delve into the past the more of its great religious periods we encounter. And it was Buddhism we revived, not the painting of the neighbouring period. So then it was a matter of finding out how something

that was the expression of a supreme value, for example Buddhist figuration, came to be a figuration governed by the supreme values of Buddhism and not by the outward appearance of the man next door, even though he may be our 'neighbor in god'. Then it is a matter of finding out how we for our part have transformed all those forms, originally created in the service of various supreme values, in order to gather them all together in the service of . . . what? That is the question. I wrote that we are the first civilization for which art falls into the province of the problematic and not of aesthetics. An art of beauty, of the cosmos, implies an aesthetic. The art of a time that has acquired a Museum without Walls, that is, an art in which vanished values are equally present, entails the problematic. To know why you love at the same time the things you love most, that's not simple. In the beginning — in about 1920, let's say — we thought it would be simple. Just as the Middle Ages had been scorned, then re-invented, so we could re-invent a sort of universal expressionism, and sweep Antiquity out of the door. And what was called 'the Antique', Graeco-Roman art, was swept out of the door; but Greece refused to be disposed of like that, Greece is in better health than ever today. It isn't a question of just re-arranging the artistic furniture every now and then. What we are seeing is a phenomenon of civilization without precedent. I repeat: without precedent. It's the whole problem of the Spenglerian conception of art. Spengler presupposes that our culture is the same as any other, to use his terminology. But other cultures have known almost nothing about their predecessors (sometimes one: the Renaissance and Antiquity), whereas they are our life blood. The Museum without Walls is also without precedent. The Museum in Alexandria was an academy. Spengler knew his art quite well, but it wasn't his field. Art would have been a great deal more upsetting for him than the history of science or thought, because it would have forced him to face up to expressions of completely different and sometimes opposed values coexisting through metamorphosis. But the idea of metamorphosis didn't interest him much: since each of his cultures was a separate organism, it vanished forever as soon as it was replaced. Spengler was a great thinker, but all that was in 1913! That's how long ago? Sixty years . . . What a chasm! For him there was *a* problem of art, and it presented itself in terms of Impressionism. So he was quite right in saying it wasn't much of a problem. Whereas Picasso presents a very real one. Above all because of his connection with our resurrection of past civilizations, with the confrontations we have engineered between them, and also between historical civilizations and historical cultures. When we set Black art beside Sumeria, it isn't just an earlier Sumeria, it's something different. The art that will have played the most mysterious, the most

< With Alberto Giacometti

< With Marc Chagall. In the background, Chagall's design for the ceiling of the Paris Opéra

With General de Gaulle (1946)

< André Malraux (1970)

In New York (1962)

active, the most leavening rôle of all in this century — Black art — has no city, no real kingdom, no temples, no history. And it's the only one."

Silence. Those words from *La Tentation de l'Occident* came into my mind: "A great empire is passing fair, but fair also is its fall." I went on:

"Do you believe that any phenomenon could now occur capable of imparting a new impulse to our civilization, something of the same nature as the reiterated promise of our past? Bergamín seemed to be divided between pessimism and optimism, both equally cool."

"A reasonable attitude, I'd say . . . On the one hand, I perceive no ferment, no promise in the spiritual sphere. On the other, well, certainly we are experiencing developments in the material and scientific sphere such as humanity has never known. But as I said before: what great advantage is there in going to the moon if it's just in order to kill ourselves off? But then again, and this is the optimistic side, no profound change of a spiritual order has ever been really predictable. After the Gospels, people could well have said that there had been the Biblical prophets, but when the Romans in Baiae asked themselves about the future . . ."

"Before the Gospels?"

"No, after. In about AD 200 . . . when they asked themselves what was in store, they said, more or less: the Roman Empire is done for, that's obvious, so what next? And they answered: well! we don't really know. And they agreed almost unanimously that the most likely hypothesis was Stoicism. But in fact the Painted Porch played no rôle at all, and Christianity swept the board. No one predicted Buddhism. No one predicted Islam. Doubtless it is in the nature of spiritual revolutions to be volcanic. But once they have erupted into existence the whole of the past is metamorphosed, it becomes theirs: the world changes its past."

"Do you see any premonitory signs?"

"None. But there can't be any, so that's no grounds for negative conclusions."

"There is a sense of expectation though, of great expectation."

"Yes, and there was that same expectancy in Rome too. And when the Greek king Menander called together representatives of all the great Greek and Indian schools of thought in Central Asia, the questions

169

he put to them were the really fundamental ones. In other words he was quite aware that things weren't going too well. And something of the same sort is going on today. Has been for . . . let's say ten years . . . At first, people thought it was the anxiety caused by the atomic bomb. Perhaps that is part of it, but it's not the whole answer. For ten years or so now the world has been sensing and murmuring to itself that something is about to happen in the spiritual sphere."

"A new way of seeing."

"What is going to come above all is a conscious grappling with the feeling of 'Things can't go on like this'. And it must be admitted that it will be the first time."

"It was what happened in 1968 . . ."

"The rebellion of youth is a worldwide phenomenon. Here in France, 1968 was very instructive, but there was also Japan, Holland, Munich, and Northern Italy. Not to mention California. But the big explosion, the biggest of all, occurred in Japan."

"There are many of us who look to you to give us, if not reasons for hope, then a line, I am tempted to say a direction."

"Then you are probably making a mistake. Probably what happens will have no conscious direction. We attach great importance to the idea of direction, because it has played a great rôle in the past. But there are certain periods when things are profoundly transformed of their own accord, assuming new forms that develop of themselves, rather like crystals. The heads of the great religions have a directive rôle. Which tends to make us think: is there a Gospel or isn't there? Is there a Koran or isn't there? Look at the eighteenth century: what crystallized in the early nineteenth century, and gave us not only the haunting discovery of history but also scientific thought, etc.; that didn't come from Voltaire, or Rousseau, or Goethe."

"Nevertheless, your life and your work are there, and a new generation is turning to them for guidance."

"Well, why not? As well that as anything else . . ."

"Do you feel yourself involved in this sense of expectation?"

"Not much. I always feel involved in any human relationship, whether personal or impersonal. I don't have a personal relationship with the Compagnons de la

< In Moscow (1968)

André Malraux and Chou En-Lai (1965)

Résistance, to whom I am due to speak next Sunday, but I do have a human relationship, and I do feel strongly involved. But in the realm of . . . let's say the mind, not particularly. I think it's the religious thinkers that feel themselves most involved in the area you're talking about. Valéry was indifferent to what came of his thinking, yet it was not negligible! Nietzsche attached great importance to the fact of thinking, but as to what effect his thought had, I wonder . . . He was pleased with that Brandès article . . . But a great religious mind must necessarily want to convey a truth. A great thinker of a non-religious kind isn't offering the world that kind of truth. You would be no more inclined than I am to apply one and the same word to the statement 'God is love' and to the formula for energy. And to say that $E = MC_2$ is a discovery whereas the Gospels are an invention would be shallow in the extreme. The prophet cannot be a prophet unless he has first detected in humanity the area that is going to prove vulnerable to his teachings, and that is exactly what makes him a prophet."

"You have taken an extremely active part in twentieth-century history, up until the departure of General de Gaulle. Do you feel now that you are parting company from history? That history, politics, the life of the city in which you have played your part, that you have helped run, in which you have held great responsibility, is a thing that no longer concerns you?"

"There isn't any."

"There isn't any?"

"Any life of the city, not at this moment. You know that as well as I do. A few years ago there was a fair amount of hope for the future, a great many enemies, it added up to a whole, back in General de Gaulle's time; since then, nothing is happening any more. And nothing is happening in the world as a whole either. Sometimes a single historical will is sufficient to create chain reactions; from the outbreak of the Spanish Civil War up to the end of the cold war, half the world lived in a state of historical will. For the moment, that's all over. There is still something happening in China, but even that is just a continuation. And here and there you get the occasional coup d'état, also inherited from the past. The world scarcely spared a glance for the tragedy in Biafra, or the one in Bangla Desh (though it's true we sell Mirages to Pakistan). Russia is in the process of becoming a big business organization. America (since the end of the Vietnam affair, a true historical event) is in the process of dissociating itself from the State. The American reality remains very powerful, but it has become detached from the scaffolding provided by

< At La Lanterne, a villa in Versailles, owned by the government and put at Malraux's disposal while he was Minister of Culture; at the time of the publication of *Antimémoires* (1967)

UDR demonstration, 1968

The author at work (1967) >

André Malraux (1972) >

177

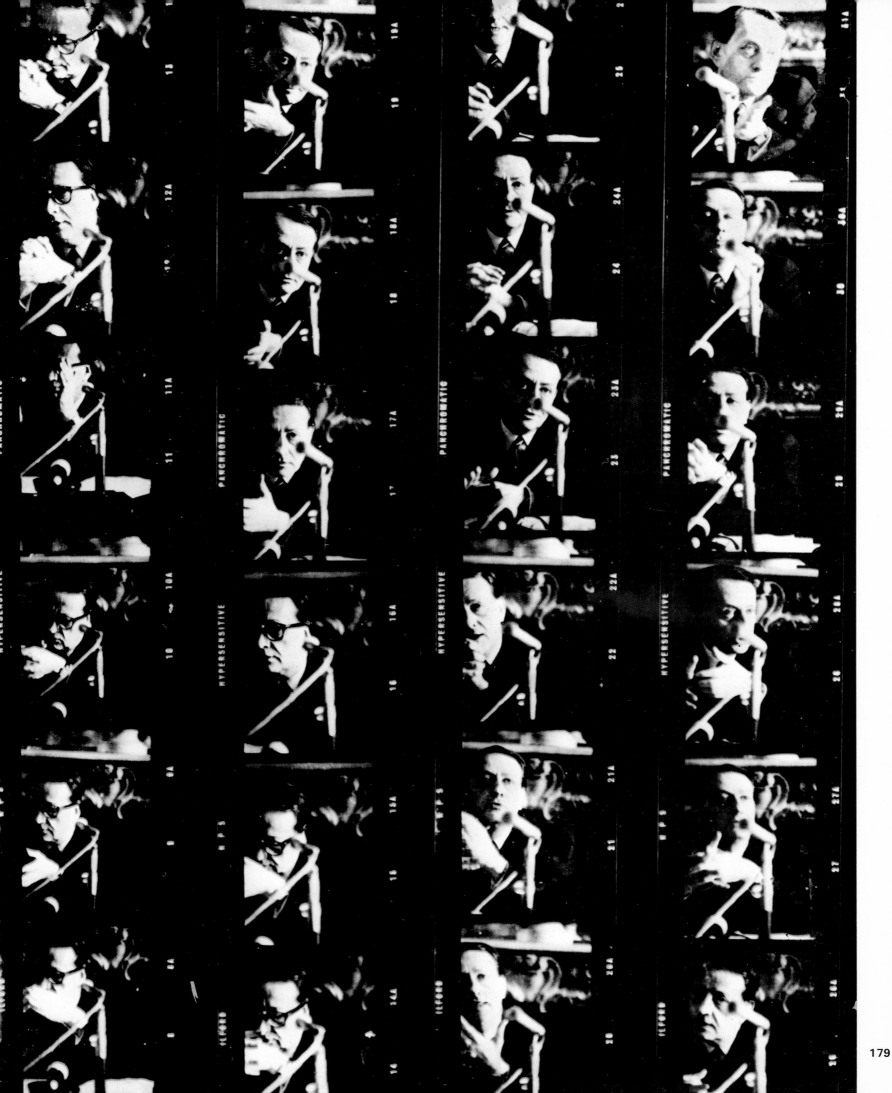

Government with a capital ·G, which is what creates order in the State, whether it's left-wing or right. It's the same problem as that of the young artists. You asked me: who are the young painters, the young writers. Remember that when the writers of my generation were twenty-five, Gallimard was making his living out of the public's excitement over what the young were *going* to do. Grasset got his publishing house going on the strength of contracts with fellows still under thirty. When Montherlant wrote his second book (the first, in those days, was always just a matter of getting a writer settled in), its publication had the same importance as that of the latest book by some famous writer. What book by a young person today would be guaranteed, in advance, the same readership as a new book by Sartre?"

"You said that Russia was becoming like a big business organization. It seems to me that the courageous voices now being raised there are the sign of a 'liberation' that the authorities can no longer control, that the authorities can no longer prevent. Solzhenitsyn and Sakharov seem to be the proof of that."

"I don't know. Solzhenitsyn is certainly a man of very great character. But as far as the Party is concerned, the situation seems to me to be this: Russia wants a *rapprochement* with the West; she believes or knows that politically she no longer has anything to fear, and a great deal to gain, by coming to terms. In which case she will have to open herself up to a technological collaboration with the West, something she is now determined to do. But the West thinks that because Russia is coming to terms, that means she will become more liberal. Whereas the Soviet government thinks that the more it opens Russia up, the greater the risk they run, and consequently the more they must crack down on the dissidents."

"That's what Sakharov predicts."

"The dissidents, who are aware of all this, see it as placing an even greater responsibility on them than ever; with the result that it is precisely now, today, that they want to make sure they are heard. And what is the consequence? That the more cordially the world powers embrace one another the more wary the Russian government becomes of Solzhenitsyn. Whereas the French firmly believed that the more Pompidou threw his arms round Brezhnev the better things would be for Solzhenitsyn. Wrong! But the Russians can't go on playing that game forever. Not while they are also trying to keep on good terms with the parties of Americans coming over to solve their wheat problem for them. Eventually, either they will have to keep the Westerners in Russia

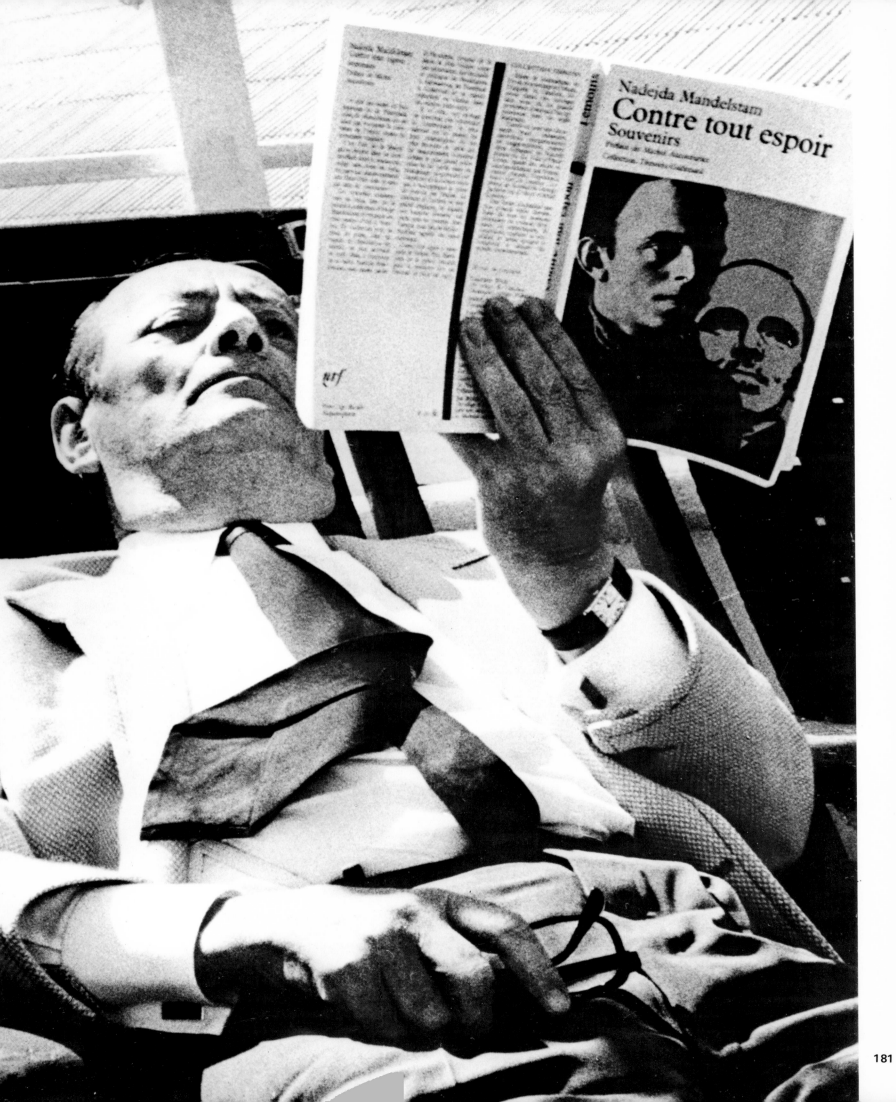

Nadejda Mandelstam
Contre tout espoir
Souvenirs

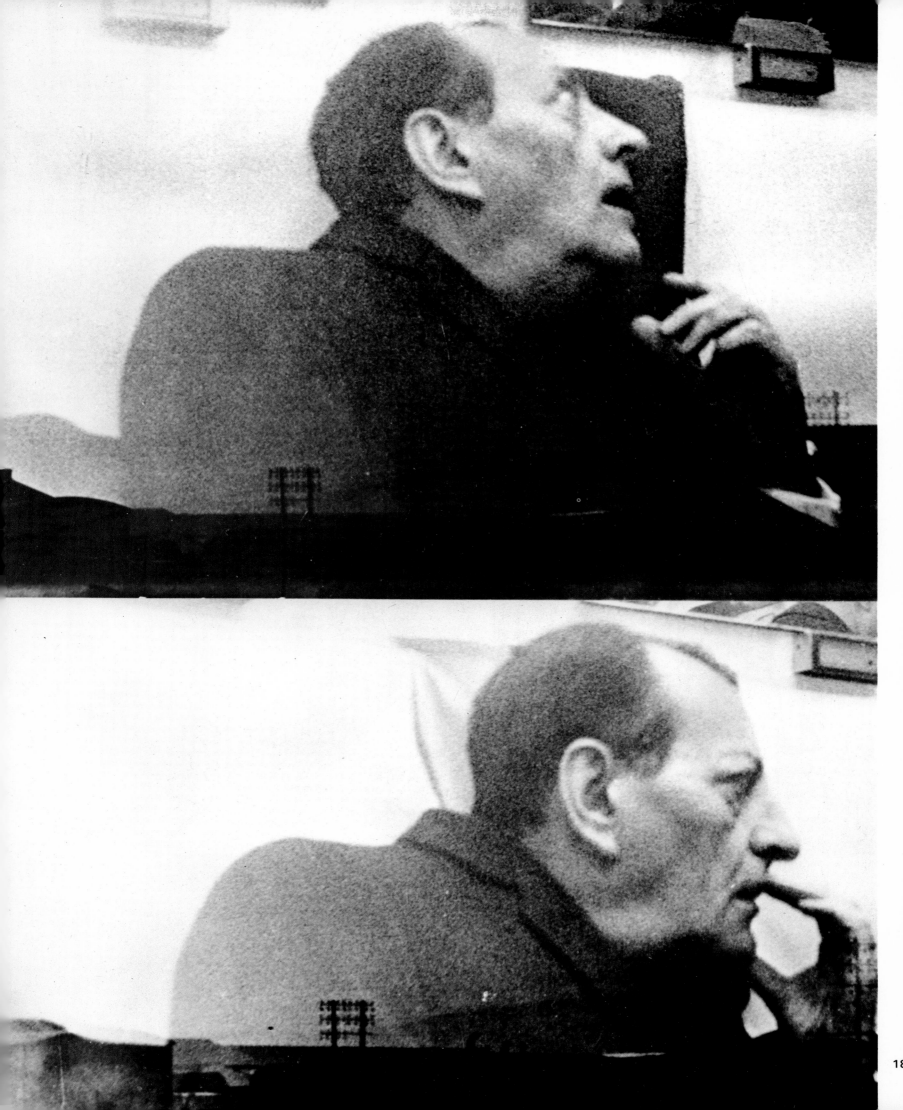

totally isolated from their own people (which wouldn't be hard; it was done in China once); or else they will have to become genuinely more liberal. The odds on either hypothesis are about even."

"And where does China fit into all this?"

"For the next fifteen years that isn't a question of much importance. Since China finally beat the problem of famine, her primary objective has been to establish a reasonable minimum living standard. That's more important than anything. When people died of hunger, they died; but now that they have new hope, if the government doesn't do everything it can in that direction, then anything else they do will be pure frivolity. That was one of the causes of the cultural revolution. Mao is determined to see that China has a certain minimum standard of living before he dies; compared with that, nothing else counts. It is likely that the standard of living is going to become the number one political question throughout the world, the question that will govern all the others. But the day the Chinese government decides that the question has been solved, then it will be just the same as it is in Russia. You don't eat too well on the collective farms, but there are the sputniks up there all the same. Though that is a situation becoming common all over the world now. In India, the reporters used to ask me: 'Why is it that you are all so excited about the Chinese, you Europeans? You live in democracies, you ought to be much more interested in us. After all, you're not Communists! Why has no one in Europe written about the fact that we are now the second largest producer of electricity in the world?' They've become the second largest producer of electricity in the world, yet they still haven't solved the problem of the untouchables. And India isn't a totalitarian state."

"Do you think the protests of non-Communist intellectuals against what is going on in Czechoslovakia or Russia are the product of a myth or the result of genuine anxiety?"

"The result of genuine anxiety. Only what bothers me — and this in no way affects the nobility and courage of the Russian dissidents — is that there is perhaps something absurd in the position of their government."

"Why absurd?"

"If it became more liberal, then Solzhenitsyn, instead of publishing an appeal that is suppressed in the Soviet Union and lauded to the skies in the West, would simply publish an article in his local equivalent of *Figaro*, not *Pravda*, that would be going too far! but in

< Boarding the train going to Colombey-les-Deux-Églises for General de Gaulle's burial (1970)

At the grave of John Fitzgerald Kennedy

André Malraux in his ministerial motorcar >

Izvestia, for example. And so?"

"You mean it wouldn't change anything?"

"Nothing. The problem they worry about was crucial during the Stalin era, when terror played a very important rôle indeed; because a relative terror is no terror at all. So Stalin was obliged to remain, as he put it, 'extremely vigilant'. But when I was in Moscow in 1966 the terror was over. What had survived was a victorious, powerful, totalitarian government obsessively concerned with trivial details of outward conformity . . . After six months the articles would possibly not be important any more . . ."

"Isn't it possible to envisage this impending Russo-American marriage of convenience inevitably modifying both their social systems? Capitalism and Socialism will be forced to cohabit. I read recently that Russia bought a quantity of American wheat, then resold it later to Italy at a considerable profit. I know, of course, that Communist doctrine doesn't wholly exclude profit, but that kind of speculation on their part — because the profit was huge — makes the mind boggle rather all the same."

"I doubt if it's true. I think they probably did use the wheat. What happened, I imagine, is that part of it didn't get distributed, because that's still an Achilles heel with them. And if they made a profit from the resale, as you were told, it wasn't because they'd suddenly become brilliant brokers but because prices had gone up in the meantime. One has to check these things."

"But the concept of profit, with all that it entails, remains the same, in West and East alike."

"Yes. But I really don't see why Communism shouldn't become reconciled to the fact of profit. It certainly wouldn't be sufficient in itself to re-establish capitalism! The fundamental idea of Marxism is in no way the elimination of profit, it is collective ownership of the means of production. Your first question was: what would happen if the Soviet Union and the United States were joined in marriage? One can conceive of their relations being similar to those between Protestantism and Catholicism after the Council of Trent. It would be rather tricky working out the practical details (the relations between Catholicism and Protestantism weren't always simple), but it could happen. The American experts would come home from Russia exactly as ours come home from Brazil, or Iran, or India. The Russians are Communists, let no one try to tell us anything to the contrary. They'd start to hear how much nicer the bathtubs are in the United States, and then another group of newspapers would say no it's not true, and the Russians would of course decide to believe them, because no country likes foreigners to have better bathtubs than its own. It wouldn't be very dramatic, it might even work very well . . . What's serious is the will towards conflict. Given the resources of modern super-States, if there's a will towards a mutual understanding then terms can always be arranged. There are never that many experts. So all that is really involved is a contagion of ideas. But the Russian government has inherited a sort of anxiety neurosis in that sphere from Stalin. Is there something deep down — this is the question you were asking just now — is there something fermenting deep down in the nature of a collective anguish? That is a question worth attention. Yet it is only by exploding into action that such anguish ever reveals its nature, and meanwhile it remains impossible to discern any difference between a daily blah-blah-blah of protest and a ferment as profound as the one that gave birth to Christianity."

Silence fell, and this time remained unbroken. Was it the silence that enabled me to return to what we have agreed to call reality?

Time slowly began again. The voice that had led me down into the essence of things was silent.

Shadows and a double silence.

So who was murmuring:

Solitude, my mother, tell me my life again!
Here is
The Wall without a crucifix and the table and the
  book lying
Closed! If the impossible so long yearned for
Tapped at the window, like a robin with a frozen
  heart,
Who would get up to let it in?[1]

[1]O. V. L. Miloscz, *Symphonie de Septembre*, Paris (n.d.).

With the river Indre its only witness in the forest's heart, summer celebrates its fiery wedding with the fall. The flames flicker in a frenzy of roaring autumn tints. Nobility and solemnity of something preparing to vanish in a final, searing explosion.

Two voices are heard through the spreading splendour.

"Metamorphosis!" says the first.

And the other adds:

"'Mysterious' metamorphosis!"

If these conversations, born of long hope, illustrated with documents that tell in parallel the story of a life, were to contribute in the eyes of the rising generation to "rousing the man of freedom against the man of fate", then my purpose, which was at no point a critical one, will have been achieved. My meetings with André Malraux and José Bergamín have dulled neither doubt nor anguish. They have nevertheless confirmed for me an essential and ineluctable truth: We are summoned.

André Malraux/Biography

1901

Georges André Malraux born in Paris 3 November. On his father's side the family was originally Flemish, his grandfather a shipowner at Dunkirk, already ruined. His father was in charge of the Paris agency of an American bank. His grandfather died in an accident in 1909. His father served in the Tank Corps during the First World War and committed suicide in 1930.

Malraux attended the Lycée Condorcet but did not finish his secondary education.

1919

Archaeological and oriental studies at the Musée Guimet and at the Louvre school, and worked in the bookshop of René-Louis Doyon.

1920

Published his first articles in Doyon's journal *La Connaissance*, then worked for the journal *Action*.

1921

Became literary director in the firm of Simon Kra (éditions du Sagittaire). At that time published Reverdy, Jarry, Max Jacob. Thanks to the support of the dealer Kahnweiler, he published his first book *Lunes en papier*. On 21 October married Clara Goldschmidt, daughter of a stockbroker. He travelled, dabbled in the market, lost, wrote for the N.R.F., met Picasso, Derain.

1923

Financially ruined, he decided to go to Cambodia. In December, reached the pagoda of Banteaï Srei, and removed some of its high reliefs. He was arrested at Pnom Penh with his friend Louis Chevasson; they were charged with theft. In 1924 given three years' prison sentence, appealed. The literary world of Paris intervened; in October the trial was reviewed, resulting in a suspended sentence. On his return to France he succeeded in having the sentence quashed.

1925

Returned to Indo-China and founded with Paul Monin the journal *L'Indochine*, which fought against the landowning colonials and the injustices of the colonial system towards the Annamites. He had the support of the Cochin-Chinese section of the Kuomintang but in August all printing facilities were closed to him and *L'Indochine* had to cease publication. Went to Hong Kong, then to Canton, to buy printing equipment. He is supposed to have assumed at Canton for some time the functions of deputy propaganda commissar to the Kuomintang, along with Borodine. Returned to Indo-China in November and began reissuing his journal under the title *L'Indochine enchaînée*.

Falling ill, he left Indo-China at the end of the year; the journal continued for a while to appear under the direction of Nguyen Pho, founder of the "Jeune Annam" movement.

1926

In Paris, he was in charge of the series "A la sphère", which published texts by Morand, Gide, Giraudoux and Mauriac. In August Grasset published *La Tentation de l'Occident* in their famous series "Cahiers verts".

He worked for various journals (*Commerce*, *Revue 600*) and Gaston Gallimard put him in charge, at the N.R.F., of books and art exhibitions.

1928

Les Conquérants suddenly had a great success.

1930

Publication of *La Voie royale*. Travels to India, Japan and the United States.

1931

Trotsky-Malraux dispute in the N.R.F. over *Les Conquérants*. Malraux returned to China.

1933

Received the Prix Goncourt for *La Condition humaine*.

1934

The Communist Party asked Malraux and André Gide to deliver a petition to Hitler's government against the detention of Dimitrov.

Malraux presided over the world committee for the liberation of Dimitrov and Thaelmann, took part in the founding of the International League against Anti-Semitism.

In February flew with Corniglion Molinier to Yemen in search of the ancient capital of the Queen of Sheba, and wrote a report of this for *l'Intransigeant*. On the return trip, the plane was caught in a storm near Bône (Algeria), an incident which he was to use in *le Temps du mépris*, *les Noyers de l'Altenburg* and his *Anti-mémoires*. Took part in the conference of Soviet writers in Moscow, where he met Gorky and Eisenstein.

1935
Took part in the international conference of writers for the defense of culture in Paris; published *Le Temps du mépris*, made the acquaintance of T. E. Lawrence and began his *Psychologie de l'Art*.

1936
Took part in the international conference of writers in London, then went to Spain very soon after Franco's military putsch. Created the España squadron, which played a role in the battles of Medellin, Toledo, Madrid and Teruel. He flew 65 missions and was wounded twice.

1937
Undertook propaganda trips to solicit funds for Republican Spain, notably to the United States, and published *L'Espoir*.

1938
Began filming of *Sierra de Teruel.*

1939
Published his first works on art. Had to interrupt filming in Catalonia because of the advancing armies of General Franco.

He finished the film but the censor prevented its showing. The war broke out and Malraux enlisted in the Tank Corps as a private.

1940
Saw action in tank battles, was taken prisoner, escaped in November and returned to the free zone. Wrote to de Gaulle to enlist in the Free French Air Force, but the person to whom he had given the letter was arrested by the Germans and had to swallow it. He had no great belief in the efficacy of the resistance movement inside France, worked at his *Psychologie de l'Art* and wrote *La Lutte avec l'Ange.*

1943
He drafted a work on T. E. Lawrence, of which only a single chapter is known. The Germans looted his library and destroyed this manuscript — *La Lutte avec l'Ange.* Only the first part of it had been published in Switzerland under the title *Les Noyers de l'Altenburg.*

He had already entered the Resistance under the name of Berger.

1944
He coordinated the Maquis of Lot, the Dordogne and La Corrèze, was wounded and arrested by the Germans on 23 July and came before the Gestapo at Toulouse. His dossier was confused with that of his brother (who was deported and died in a concentration camp). He was liberated by the Allied troops, created the Alsace-Lorraine Brigade which he directed under the name of 'Colonel Berger' and took part in the battles of Sainte-Odile, Mulhouse and Strasbourg. His second wife, Josette Clotis, was killed in an accident.

1945
Attended the congress of the National Liberation Movement, calling for the nationalization of the banks. His unit crossed the Rhine, entered Stuttgart and Nuremberg. He refused to join the intellectuals' group around Sartre who were founding *Les Temps modernes*; in June he met de Gaulle for the first time and in August was named the general's technical adviser. Then in November appointed Minister of Information.

1946
Resigned at the same time as de Gaulle, published *Scènes choisies*, extracts from his works, and in November he called an important conference at the Sorbonne on man and artistic culture.

1947
Took part in the founding of the R.P.F. (*Rassemblement du Peuple Français*) of which he became delegate for propaganda, and gave a certain number of political lectures. Published his essays on art in Geneva.

1948
Founded a journal, *le Rassemblement*, was actively engaged in politics and married the pianist Madeleine Lioux, widow of his brother who died after being deported.

1949
Founded *Liberté de l'esprit*, managed by Claude Mauriac. The R.P.F., which had achieved in 1948 a great success in the municipal elections, lost votes in the cantonal elections.

1950
Gravely ill. Published *Saturne.*

1951
Failure of the R.P.F. in the legislative elections, publication of *Les Voix du silence*, revised and enlarged text of *La Psychologie de l'Art.*

1952
Gave a lecture at the Congress for the Freedom of Culture.

1953
End of the R.P.F. Malraux pursued his work and publications on art.

1954
Supported the Mendès-France government while continuing to call himself a Gaullist. Thierry Maulnier adapted *La Condition humaine* for the theater.

1958
Malraux, Martin du Gard, Mauriac and Sartre "summon the public powers in the name of the declaration of the rights of man and the citizen to condemn without qualification the use of torture which dishonours the cause it seeks to serve". Total war in Algeria. 13 May in Algiers: de Gaulle returned to power. Malraux named ministerial deputy to the President of the Council. He reiterated his position against torture, and suggested naming a commission to enquire into this subject in Algeria. This commission never left France.

He gave a number of political lectures in France and abroad, met Nehru.

1959
Became Minister of Cultural Affairs.

1960
Following the suppression of *La Gangrène*, which gave proof of the practice of torture in Algeria and France, 121 intellectuals, among them Sartre, signed an appeal calling on French soldiers to refuse obedience; Malraux attacked Sartre violently even though he recognized the existence of torture.

Lecture on the preservation of monuments in Nubia. Travels.

1961
Malraux reacted violently to the putsch of the rebel generals in Algiers, and called on the French to form armed militias to resist them. His two sons killed in an automobile accident.

1962
O.A.S. attempt on his life. He escaped injury, but a little girl was gravely wounded. He welcomed the Evian agreements and founded the Association for the Fifth Republic.

1963
Sent the *Mona Lisa* to New York. Various lectures on art and politics.

1964
Speech in favour of transferring Jean Moulin's ashes to the Panthéon. Opened the first Maison de la Culture.

1965
After an illness, left for the Far East. On the ship he began the writing of his *Antimémoires*. Met Mao Tse-Tung to whom he gave a message from General de Gaulle. Made a speech at the Palais des Sports in support of the re-election of de Gaulle as president.

1966
Inaugurated the world festival of Black art at Dakar and the Picasso exhibition in Paris.

1967
Published the first volume of his *Antimémoires*.

1968
Gave a speech at the Parc des Expositions on the student revolt: "We are not up against the need for reforms, but one of the deepest crises that civilization has ever known".

1969
Malraux retired at the same time as de Gaulle. Along with Mauriac and Sartre, demanded that the Bolivian government free Régis Debray.

1970
Present at Colombey-les-Deux-Eglises for de Gaulle's funeral. He had seen de Gaulle in his own home a few months before.

1971
Published an account of this interview under the title *Les Chênes qu'on abat*. Supported the movement for Bengali autonomy against Pakistan.

Went to Bengal in 1973. Worked on the second volume of *Antimémoires*. Published *Les Oraisons funèbres*.

1972
Françoise Verny and Claude Santelli made a series of films about and with Malraux for the O.R.T.F., under the title *La Légende du siècle*.

1973
Preface to *Le Clou brûlant* by José Bergamín.

1974
The N.R.F. announces *La Tête d'obsidienne*.

André Malraux/Bibliography

1920
Des origines de la poésie cubiste (journal *La Connaissance*).

1921
Lunes en papier (pub. Galerie Simon).

1922
Ecrit pour une idole à trompe (mimeograph).
Les Hérissons apprivoisés and *Journal d'un pompier de jeu de massacre* (journal *Les Signaux de France et de Belgique*).

1923
Preface to *Mademoiselle Monk*, by Charles Maurras.

1926
La Tentation de l'Occident (Grasset); English language editions *The Temptation of the West* (New York 1961, London 1968).

1927
Ecrit pour un ours en peluche (Revue 600).
Le Voyage aux îles Fortunées (journal *Commerce*).
D'une jeunesse européenne, in 'Ecrits', collective work (Grasset).

1928
Les Conquérants (Grasset); English language editions *The Conquerors* (New York and London 1929).
Royaume farfelu (Gallimard).

1930
La Voie royale (Grasset); English language editions *The Royal Way* (New York and London 1935).

1931
Exposition gréco-bouddhique.
Exposition gothico-bouddhique (N.R.F.).
Discussions Trotsky-Malraux (N.R.F.).

1932
Œuvres gothico-bouddhiques du Pamir (N.R.F.).
Jeune Chine (N.R.F.).

Exhibition of works by Sémirani (N.R.F.).
Preface to *Lady Chatterley's Lover* by D. H. Lawrence (Gallimard).

1933
Exposition Fautrier (N.R.F.).
Preface to *Sanctuary* by William Faulkner (Gallimard).
La Condition humaine (Gallimard); English language editions *Storm in Shanghai* (London 1934); *Man's Fate* (New York 1934); *Man's Estate* (London 1948).

1934
Lettre à Goebbels.
Le Royaume de Saba (articles in *L'Intransigeant*).

1935
Le Temps du mépris (Gallimard); English language editions *Days of Wrath* (New York 1936); *Days of Contempt* (London 1936).
Preface to *Indochine S.O.S.*, by Andrée Viollis (Gallimard).

1937
L'Espoir (Gallimard); English language editions *Man's Hope* (New York 1938); *Days of Hope* (London 1938).

1938
Writings on art (*Verve*): *La Psychologie des renaissances, De la représentation en Orient et en Occident.*
Laclos in *Tableau de la littérature française* (Gallimard).

1939
Sierra de Teruel (film).

1943
La Lutte avec L'Ange (1st part: *Les Noyers de l'Altenburg*, Editions du Haut-Pays, Lausanne).
Le Camp de Chartres (Fontaine, Algiers).

1946
N'était-ce donc que cela? single chapter of *Démon de l'Absolu* (Editions du Pavé).
Esquisse d'une psychologie du cinéma (Gallimard).
Scènes choisies, extracts from his novels (Gallimard).

Les Noyers de l'Altenburg (Gallimard); English language edition *The Walnut Trees of Altenburg* (London 1955).

1947
Dessins de Goya au musée du Prado (Skira).
Le Musée imaginaire (1st volume of *La Psychologie de l'Art*, Skira); English language editions *Museum without Walls* (New York and London 1949).

1948
La Création artistique (2nd volume of *La Psychologie de l'Art*, Skira); English language editions *The Creative Act* (New York and London 1949).

1949
La Monnaie de l'Absolu (3rd volume of *La Psychologie de l'Art*, Skira); English language editions *Twilight of the Absolute* (New York and London 1951).

1950
Saturne (Gallimard); English language editions *Saturn, an essay on Goya* (New York and London 1957).
Nous l'aimions, text on Léo Lagrange (La Compagnie du livre).

1951
Les Voix du silence (Gallimard). English language editions *The Voices of Silence* (New York and London 1954).

1952
First volume of *Musée imaginaire de la sculpture mondiale* (Gallimard).
Prefaces to *Van Gogh et les peintres d'Auvers chez le docteur Gachet* (L'Amour de l'Art);
to *Tout l'œuvre peint de Leonard de Vinci*;
to *Tout Vermeer de Delft*;
to *Barrès parmi nous*, by P. de Boisdeffre;
to *Qu'une larme dans l'océan*, by Manès Sperber (Calmann-Lévy).

1953
Preface to *Chimères ou Réalités*, by General Jacquot (Gallimard).

1954
Volumes 2 and 3 of *Musée imaginaire de la sculpture mondiale*:
– *Des bas-reliefs aux grottes sacrées*;
– *Le monde chrétien*.
Prefaces to *Saint-Just ou la Force des choses*, by Albert Olivier (Gallimard);
to *Sang noir*, by Louis Guilloux (Gallimard);
to *Israël*, album of photos by Izis (Clairefontaine, Lausanne).

1957
La Métamorphose des Dieux (Gallimard); English language editions *The Metamorphosis of the Gods* (New York and London 1960).

1960
Preface to *Sumer*, by André Parot (Gallimard).

1967
Antimémoires (Gallimard); English language editions *Antimemoirs* (New York and London 1968).
10 Discours de Malraux (journal *Renaissance 2000* no. 5).

1970
Le Triangle noir (Gallimard).

1971
Oraisons funèbres (Gallimard).
Les Chênes qu'on abat (Gallimard); English language edition *Fallen Oaks* (New York and London 1972).

José Bergamín/Biography

José Bergamín was born in 1895 in Madrid where he spent his childhood and youth. The first literary friendships linked him to Perez de Ayala, Salinas Gomez de la Serna and all the generation of 27: Antonio Espina, García Lorca, Gerardo Diego, Alberti, Alfonso Reyes.

In 1923 Juan Ramon Jimenez published Bergamín's first book, *The Fuse and the Star*. Also dating from this period are *Three Scenes at Right Angles* (1924), *Characters* (1926), *The Enemy who Flees* (1927). In 1933 he directed the series 'Cruz y Raya' in which he began to publish his *Disparadero Espagnol*. The Civil War was the beginning of a long exile for him. He went to Mexico first, where he published *The Pit of Anguish* (1941), *The Passenger*, *A Spanish Pilgrim in America* and *The Extinguished Voice* (1943), and *The Daughter of God* in 1945. He then went to Venezuela and Uruguay, where he published among others *Melusine and the Mirror* (1952), *Medea the Enchantress* (1954). He lived in Paris from 1954 to 1958, the year when he returned to Spain, from which he was expelled in 1963. It was not until 1970 that he was permitted to return.

Sources of illustrations

Archives André Malraux: 11, 13, 14, 15, 21, 23, 24, 26–27, 29, 30–31, 32, 35, 40, 47, 56–57, 66–67, 69, 70, 73, 86–87, 89, 101, 102, 105, 106, 118, 120, 121, 129, 140, 150, 158, 159, 160, 162
Archives Clara Malraux: 39, 64, 110–11
Gilles Caron/Gamma: 176
Chang-Pin/China Photo Service: 173
J. C. Deutsch: 181
Dorka: 165
Dourdin/Rapho: 178, 184
G. Freund: 96, 123, 174–75
Habans/Paris-Match: 166–67
Ph. Halsman: 144
G. Krull: 58
Life: 138
Ralph Morse: 117
L. Nau: 170–71
R. Parry: 48
Photo-Izis: 163
Photo Leirens: 61
Potier/Paris-Match: 151
Press Information: 157
Daniel Pype: 18–19, 36–37, 44–45, 98–99, 114–15, 134–35
M. Roy: 152, 168
Thouvenin: 17
Vals/Paris-Match: 179
Roger Viollet: 51, 109
Wurtz/Paris-Match: 182, 183, 186–87